FISHERMAN

FISHERMAN

The Strife And Times Of Ronald K. Peterson Of Ballard

George Lowe

To order additional copies of this book, contact:
Xlibris Corporation
1-888-795-4274
www.Xlibris.com
Orders@Xlibris.com
18538

TO THE BELOVEDS—ALDENE, AMY, SCOTT, MARIANNE, PERLA, MAX, ISABEL AND OONA.

CHAPTER 1

"He was strong and bold and there was a great deal
of goodness in him, even though he had the mischief that
has to go with sailing on the sea, which he did. And he
was a fisherman."
—from a Gaelic legend as told to John McNulty

Fifty-two year old Ronald K. Peterson, who bears a passing resemblance to Elvis Presley, is a hard-bellied six-foot-five who can still bench press 190 pounds ten times straight. His face is a roadmap of fist fights, accidents and strenuous outdoor living. How Presley might have looked had he turned to boxing or pro football instead of music.

Peterson lives in Seattle. Around town, he wears Levis and cowboy boots, with a leather-sleeved black warm-up jacket that has a portrait of his crab boat, *Aleutian Number One*, embroidered across the back. The years he spent shouting to be heard over the racket of big diesel engines have left him with a voice as strong as his handshake. He has a shock of black hair that keeps falling in his eyes and employs a startling pop-eyed stare for conversational emphasis. Despite his somewhat forceful appearance, Peterson is as friendly, enthusiastic and gregarious as a black Labrador puppy. A great big one.

I had not seen him for a couple of years when he showed up one noon in the winter of 1998 at Bad Albert's, a workingman's tavern in Seattle's Ballard neighborhood, where I was having lunch with a friend. Ron had dropped off a repair job at Broomfield's Welding next door and had come over with Ed Broomfield, the owner, to grab a sandwich.

"Sit down, join us, what's new?"

Quite a bit as it turned out.

Ron said, yeah, he still owned the *Aleutian Number One*, his 126-foot Marco crab boat which he and two partners bought in 1978. He also still owned and fished the *Brianne Lynn*, his 32-foot aluminum Bristol Bay gillnetter, and now had a half interest in another. He had recently invested $1.5 million in the *Akutan*, an old 177-foot processor which he wanted to refit and use to process crab and salmon and longline for cod. But there was a big fight with the feds, the state and the bank over the vessel's permits and there was also a bitter legal battle with an insurance company that had defaulted on a $250,000 claim for fire damage on the boat while it was in the yard. He had recently taken an option to buy a waterfront processing plant in Anacortes, a town about 75 miles north of Seattle. He was putting together another Bristol Bay co-op venture which he hoped to develop into a vertically integrated fishing and processing company. While he had cut back on most of his industry association activities, he was still on the board of three private fishboat insurance pools in Ballard as well as the Alaska Crab Coalition, an outfit that he helped organize in 1984 to combat the draggers laying waste to the Bering Sea King crab grounds. And his seventeen-year-old son—as most 17-year-old sons are—was still a big worry and pretty much as rambunctious as Ron himself had been at that age.

And oh yes, his wife Gloria had just divorced him after 24 years of marriage.

"It's been a little crazy," said Ron.

I first met Peterson at Ray's Boathouse on Shilshole Bay back in the early 1980's. The upstairs bar commands a sweeping westward view of Puget Sound, the Olympics and the channel leading to the Ballard Locks. Every fishboat, tug or yacht going in or out of Salmon Bay, Lake Union, Portage Bay or Lake Washington passed right in front of the bar, so the scenery, the marine traffic and the broken-wristed bartender made late afternoon at Ray's a pleasant venue indeed. I was a Ray's regular at the time, although this was near the tail end of my own sport drinking days. The place attracted an interesting cross section of patrons including contractors, insurance brokers, carpenters, a UW professor or two and a number of crab fishermen and fishing industry characters. Conversations were generally amusing and occasionally informative.

Ron came up that day with Gloria, in tow. An absolutely stunning and charming brunette, she had to be the prettiest girl to graduate from Grays Harbor High School in the last half century. From the joshing which greeted them as they came into the bar, it was clear that former All-Pro Hell-Raiser Ron Peterson had settled down. With a wife and two kids, he had become a solid citizen and his wild days were behind him. "They used to say you weren't really a man unless you drank. Now it's more like you're not a man if you can't quit."

I kept bumping into Peterson around town as the years rolled on. In 1990 I made a short documentary about him for a local television station, part of a series about interesting Seattle people. We used his story of a near escape from drowning in Bristol Bay back in 1984.

CHAPTER 2

"1984 was the first year we had survival suits in Bristol Bay. It was at night. We were running in with the storm behind us and I'd never seen the seas so big. Our boat was overloaded—we even had fish in the cockpit. As we got into shallower water, the seas got even bigger with the wind and waves against the outgoing current and when we got near the entrance to the river channel we hit the tip of a sand bar and a couple of huge ones swamped us and the next thing I knew, the floorboards were floating off the engine room. The stern was under water and just the bow sticking out keeping us afloat. The two guys I had with me wanted to jump, but I told them that they'd drown sure if they did. The sea was so big and the wind was so high it was just a boiling mist and pretty soon I could see these quartz lights and it was like seeing God coming for you—mystical lights in the mist because it was pitch dark and the waves were so big. I couldn't actually see the boat until it got real close. It was a guy from Port Heiden, part native, who had seen our mast lights. He was the only one crazy enough to leave the harbor and come crashing out

in this storm. He got up close and by timing the surge of
the boats my guys were able to jump across to his bow. I was
waist deep in water in the cabin cramming everything I
could into my survival suit—my wallet and my fish book
and my 45 Magnum and I had so much stuff I couldn't
get through the window. So I threw it all away and
managed to worm through the window and get out on the
bow. The next time the other boat got close I jumped across
and got a handhold on their rail and they hauled me on.
I looked back and my boat was gone. The next day we flew
over and there was no trace of the boat. Not a trace. That
guy who came out to save us was really something. I offered
to buy him a case of whiskey but he wouldn't take it."

Ronnie Peterson is Ballard born and bred. And to
understand him, it helps to understand the place where he grew
up. Located at the northwest corner of Seattle, the Ballard
neighborhood is heavily Scandinavian, and really the only
remaining area of the city with a history that's continous and
coherent. It got its start as a bustling sawmill town and was a
separate municipality until annexed in 1896. (Ballard streets
originally had nautical names. "We live at the corner of Canoe
and Schooner." It got a bit confusing.) Bordered on the east by
Phinney Ridge and the west by Puget Sound, Ballard proper
runs from Salmon Bay north to about 85th street.—an area roughly
square, about two miles on each side. It's getting a bit yuppie
these days, but blue-collar Ballard is still firmly rooted in the
reality of sea and storm, risk and reward based on dangerous
work and physical discomfort.

When the first settlers came in the 1870's, Salmon Bay was a
long, shallow tidal inlet fed by five salmon-filled streams. Vast
stands of virgin fir and cedar marched up the surrounding hills.
After the nearby forests were logged, the Ballard mills were fed
by huge floating rafts of logs towed in from other parts of the
Sound to be sawed up into lumber, lath and shingles.

By 1897, the town of Ballard had thirteen sawmills, more

than either Seattle, Tacoma or Everett. By 1902, Ballard mills employed 1800 men working 10 hour shifts, Monday through Saturday, whomping out 3 million cedar shingles and some 350,000 board feet of lumber every working day. Average pay for sawmill workers was $3.50 per shift. The men in the shingle mills—"shingle weavers"—only got a dollar. Besides paying lower wages, the shingle mills were even more dangerous. The old saying ran, "Give the boss two of your fingers the day you're hired, he'll take the rest of them as he needs them." Besides their missing fingers, Ballard millworkers could be spotted by their habit of chewing Copenhagen snuff or "snoose"—the only tobacco allowed in the firetrap mills. To this day, old timers call the Ballard area Snoose Junction.

Ballard production peaked in 1910. As the region's forests became depleted, the Salmon Bay waterfront became increasingly given over to small shipyards and commercial fishing vessels as it is today The mouth of Salmon Bay was dammed by the Hiram Chittenden Locks in 1912. Then Salmon Bay, Lake Washington, Portage Bay and Lake Union were interconnected by a dredged ship canal and the levels of each body of water were equalized— Salmon Bay was raised fourteen feet, Lake Washington drawn down nine feet and Lake Union and Portage Bay lowered five. One happy result was that ships and boats could then be brought in through the locks to sit in fresh water to kill barnacles and shipworms. There were only three mills left after World War II. The Seattle Cedar Company disappeared in 1958, its towering stacks of air-drying cedar going up in the biggest bonfire the city had ever seen—so hot that it blistered paint on houses two miles away to the south on Queen Anne Hill. The Stimson Mill closed in the 1960's and the last of them, U.S. Plywood, shut down in 1984.

Today, the marine industrial area on both sides of Salmon Bay is the best place in the North Pacific for fishboats and processors to find new equipment or get things fixed. Ketchikan is technically the southernmost city in Alaska, but for all practical purposes, Alaska's real southern capital is Ballard. Since the

Cold War ended, even the Russians have started coming here for refits and new gear. Fishermen call it "The Pit" and the shores of Salmon Bay are crammed with shipyards, marine ways, industrial moorages, chandleries, machine shops, welders, electricians, hydraulic and electronic suppliers, engine companies, propellor and transmission companies, winch builders, net makers and industrial hardware stores. Anything and everything it takes to build, equip and repair any fishing vessel, tug, barge or processor from the keel to the tip of the mast. All that stuff, all those skilled trades. Rope, rust, and bilge water. Steel, machinery and welding rod.

Market Street running east and west is Ballard's main commercial street and north of Market is residential, financial, and religious. Block after block of modest wooden bungalows on small city lots, and more churches per square mile than in any other area of comparable size in the city. Many of these churches are still going strong, but there are a dozen or more old frame churches that are now residences or converted to other uses. The wives of Ballard's millworkers and fishermen obviously did a lot of praying.

The other important street is the drinking strip along treelined Ballard Avenue running at an angle from Market down to the Ballard Bridge parallel to the northern shore of Salmon Bay. Tavern after tavern, some right next door to each other. They're relics from the days when saloon licenses were easy to get and there were hordes of thirsty customers—fishermen, shipwrights and millworkers. In most of the saloons a man could get drunk on the first floor and if he had an extra dollar or two, find feminine companionship upstairs. Today, most of these old places are straight beer taverns and many have music at night attracting a young crowd. Only a handful are still heavy-duty drinking places.

Ballard is by no means as wild and wooly as it was in the old days, but there's still a fair amount of local color. Ballard Eagles for example. Ballard Elks. Ballard Sons of Norway. Ballard Masons. All the guys who own the yards and businesses along the canal on either side of Ballard Oil fight to keep the condominiums out and make it stay industrial. There's a Norwegian "Mafia" in this neighborhood for sure. Ballard used to have a Lucia Bride cellebration every spring, but although that's gone away, Settenmai, the Norwegian Independence Day, is still celebrated with a parade and there's a Seafood Fest every June with Market Street closed off and filled with booths selling "Bite of Ballard" seafood dishes.

Except for the sawmills, hardworking Ballard is pretty much what it has always been, its character is largely unchanged. Not quite as intensely Scandinavian as it once was, but still well supplied with Norwegians and Swedes with a sprinkling of Finns and Danes. The big immigration began in the 1880's. By 1910, three out of five foreign born in Ballard were Scandinavians and of these half were Norwegian. To this day, Norwegians form the largest and most cohesive ethnic group. And to this day, it is said that most people back home in Norway can readily point to Ballard on the map. Ron Peterson says that quite a few old-country Norwegian fishermen never got more than a few blocks away from Ballard except when they went to sea.

Ron grew up with a slight Norwegian accent. It's hard to describe, easy to recognize. He is well spoken and articulate, pronounces his words with easy precision (and remarkably little profanity). But his slightly different consonantal stresses and phrasings fall on the ear with a hint of Norway. In the same way that most airline pilots speak with a whiff of Right-stuff-Texan, I think that what Ron has is actually kind of an occupational accent—Ballard Fisherman.

In Seattle, the Norwegians and Swedes are regarded with affection and respect but Ballard itself gets the put-down. It's Seattle's Brooklyn, the joke neighborhood whose mention brings a condescending grin. Fortunately, Scandinavian humor is cheerfully self-deprecating. The Swedes and Norwegians kid each other about being thick. One Norwegian says to another. "Did you hear about the Norwegian who got in an accident and lost half his brain and still lived." "Oh yeah, what's he doing now?" "Teaching school in Sweden." Swedes, of course, tell it the other way around. Or the classic: "Norwegian heads are so square Ballard haircuts are priced at two-bits a side." And another: "Didja hear about the guy who got rich in Ballard selling Cheerios as doughnut seeds?" Or the story about the widow putting a funeral notice in the paper: "What do you want to say, Mrs. Olson?" asked the funeral director. "Just say 'Ole died.'" "But that's only two words, you get to use five words." "OK, then, put in there, 'Ole died, boat for sale.'"

The letter J is pronounced Y in Norwegian so "yumpin' yimminy' falls hilariously on non-Scandinavian ears. Local humorist Stan Boreson—a professional Norwegian if there ever was one—is well loved in Ballard as well as throughout Seattle. He started his accordion-playing-Norwegian-fool act while still a student at the University of Washington and went on to great success as host of a long-running afternoon children's show on local TV. Dialect songs and absolutely shameless "Uncle Torvald's-underwear" Scandinavian humor. Maybe some Norwegians got sore about it, but I never heard of any protest marches in Ballard, and in fact Boreson for many years ran a very successful music store right there on Market Street and he still parades on Settenmai.

But the really funny thing about most of the Norwegians of Ballard is how successful they have been. They don't mind poking a little fun at themselves. They can afford it.

CHAPTER 3

*"I first went fishing with my Dad when I was four
years old up in the San Juan Islands for a night or two.
Then every summer starting when I was seven gillnetting
in the San Juans and the Straits of Juan de Fuca. We'd
fish all night and during the day my Dad and I would
sleep. My Mom pitched a tent up there at McKay Harbor
on the south end of Lopez. And she cooked for us and it was
a pretty nice life"*

R on's father, Knute, came to Ballard from Norway in 1932.
Landing in New York with his older brother, Ingvold, the two
young immigrants made their way west via Canada to Vancouver,
B.C. with a one winter stopover working on an Alberta farm for
board and room. Ingvold decided to settle in Vancouver because
a fortune teller had told him he was going to marry a Canadian
girl and he figured he'd better stick around and see who she was.
Knute however, continued on to Ballard where Norwegian friends
helped him find work in a cannery.

Before long he found better pay in a lumber camp, laboring
as a choker-setter, the man whose task it was to clamber over

felled trees and attach a heavy wire cable so each log could be yarded in from where it landed. As one of the most dangerous jobs in the woods, setting choker was always one of the easiest to get.

"After three years, Dad was completely busted up from logs rolling over him," Ron recalls. "His legs looked like road maps with all the scars. After he left logging, he started a fishing career that went on another fifty years with those busted-up legs." Like many a Norwegian fisherman of his era, he couldn't swim a stroke.

Knute learned his trade on fish traps in Alaska and by crewing on halibut and cod boats fishing off the Washington coast. In 1948, the year after Ron was born, Knute bought his first boat, a 36-foot gillnetter. He fished the *Ronnie K* successfully through the fifties for salmon, cod and halibut around the Sound and the Straits of Juan de Fuca between Washington and Vancouver Island.

Ron's mother, Teofilia, was fetched over from Poland by an older sister who had come to Alaska several years earlier and married a saloon keeper and gold-mine owner in the little town of Flat near Iditarod. Teofilia worked as a cook before being brought down to Seattle by a kindly couple who thought the raucous gold camps were no place for a pretty young teenage girl. She and Knute met at a dance and were married in 1939. The Petersons eventually were able to buy a little two bedroom frame house in North Ballard where his mother still lives to this day. Ronnie was their only child. Raised in the Catholic faith, he was sent to St. Alphonsus, Ballard's one Catholic grade school.

Ron's mother was and still is a force to be reckoned with. At 87, she's a slim and handsome woman who's a good deal tougher than she looks. When he was in the third grade, Ron had a severe bout of bronchitis and for one whole year she wouldn't let him leave the house without wearing a heavy woolen coat, bright red. "The kids teased me and started calling me Ronnie Red Coat and I guess it was about then that I learned to fight." Ron's own son Kris went to live with his grandmother for a while two years ago. She kicked him out of the house one morning when he wouldn't eat his toast. When Ron started lifting weights in high school, Teofilia made fun of him and his pals one day. "You boys ought to get paid for lifting weights," she declared, and much to the chagrin of Ron's pals who were topped out with the barbell at 110 pounds, she picked it off the floor and easily hoisted it over her head. Twice.

Ron's Dad moved back to Norway in 1977. "Just told my Mom he was going out and never came back. Sent me a power of attorney in the mail and said 'You divorce her for me, I'm scared of that woman.' It was horrible. Four days in court, it was one of the hardest things I ever had to do. She gave me the toughest battle I ever had. We didn't speak for five years afterwards. I always say I'm half Klingon and she's 100 percent," Ron is a dutiful son, however, looks after her and frequently takes her to mass.

The experience of summer gillnetting in the San Juan Islands got Ronnie hooked. Setting the net at sunset, pulling the net, picking the salmon and resetting through the night, selling the fish to the buyer boat every morning, sleeping during the warm summer days. Ron not only liked the life, he liked the money. Even though his father paid him far less than a crewman's normal share, it was considerably more than his school friends earned delivering newspapers or mowing lawns. "I never wore Levis all thetime I was in high school. Slacks always, and I had a different sweater for almost every day of the month."

Ballard kids grew up hearing about fathers, brothers, uncles, cousins and their big fishing paydays. The fisherman who owned the boat may have only cleared enough for expenses, boat payments and a new dress for the Missus, but for a teenage crewmember, that end-of-season share check represented income that was fully disposable. New cars—Camaros and Mustangs especially—were a common sight around Ballard every fall. By spring most were unwashed, well-dented and needed new mufflers. A tired, twenty-five-year-old blondie with two little towheads in the backseat of a beat-up Camaro was the outcome of many a Ballard High School romance. Big summer money, slim part-time pickings the other nine months. ("When are you going to quit fishing and get a real job?")

The father, uncle or friend who owned the fish boat fully expected every member of his crew to pitch in every spring—without pay—to paint, mend nets and get everything ready to head north again. Still, going fishing was an adventure. Add the money and no wonder most Ballard kids tried to wangle their way onto a boat. Youngsters who did go fishing often came back with augmented vocabularies. I knew of one returning teenager who became increasingly embarrassed by his inability to stop using fishboat language around his family. Served lamb stew one night soon after his return from Alaska, he took one bite and said ruefully, "Aw shit, Ma, I can't eat this fucking stuff." Red faced, he jumped up and ran out of the house.

Ronnie kept fishing with his dad until he was fifteen. By that time Knute Peterson had bought a bigger boat and was fishing Southeast Alaska in the summer. Ron was doing a man's work but his dad still wouldn't pay him a full crewman's share. "He'd give me some money but I wasn't earning a paycheck. So when I was fifteen, I up and quit him and got a job seining with a guy named Dick Leese on the *Solta*. Went to Southeastern and got a full share. And Dick wanted me back. But the next year I got a job in Bristol Bay and it was the biggest year they ever had and boy, it really bit me. Big money for a kid."

"You know it's really funny," says Ron, "because I was wild and I hung around with the wild boys and a lot of them are dead now, but I went fishing every summer and I'd come back and hear all about what had gone on in Ballard and the guys wanted to know about my adventures. By the time I got out of high school, I had a '64 Pontiac two-plus-two and had made enough that season to buy *two* more fully equipped GTO's and an apartment for a year, but I didn't do it, I saved it and went to school, but that's kind of how we equated how much money we made."

Ron's parents wanted him to go to college and get an education. And despite the money he made fishing, so did Ron.

With good high school grades, he entered Seattle University where he studied Civil Engineering.

"I always had an ambition to build bridges," he says," but I finally got disenchanted with school. I got a job offer when I was a junior. The salary was something like ten grand a year and I'd have to move to Austin, Texas. Hell, I made that much every summer fishing to pay for my college."

With the Vietnamese war going on, Ron decided to go in the Army.

"I was in the ROTC but I had a low draft number so I knew I was going to have to go one way or another. So I quit school and went down and volunteered and said, 'Take me, I want to be out in May of '70 so I can go fishing.' And it worked. I was at Fort Ord in an infantry division ready to ship out to Vietnam and for some reason they said they needed two guys to go to Alaska and I knocked people down running up there to volunteer and that's where they sent me. I did two years as a company clerk at Fort Richardson in Anchorage. And I got back in '70 in time for the season. I had two thousand dollars saved and put it down on a Bristol Bay boat. It was twelve grand, spare engine, all the nets. I had to come up with the rest by August 25th. We fished for New England Fish Company, and we were on limit a lot, so we could only catch so much, but I still made $9500 in six weeks which gave me my boat almost free and clear after one year."

The Bristol Bay sockeye season only lasted from mid-June through the last weeks of July. After he got back from Bristol Bay that year, Ron found work as the bouncer at the Sands Tavern, Ballard's go-go joint eight blocks up the street from the high school. "Me and 20 dancers. I thought I had died and gone to heaven. But it was too dangerous. They told me never to leave the bar and that was the right advice. One of the bartenders went out back one night and a bunch of bikers carved him up so bad he needed 250 stitches. No future in that business."

Figuring fishing as a marginally safer if less romantic profession, Ron leased a little Puget Sound gillnetter for a year and made enough to buy one outright in Canada for $6000 the following year. "I made a pretty good living just fishing those little boats in Puget Sound and then fishing Bristol Bay in the summer. And then I'd go shrimping in the winter, and go crabbing sometimes, and it kind of worked out."

There were a lot of salmon still left in Puget Sound during the 70's. Ron tells of gillnetting out of the Shilshole Bay Marina. "Dad and I would hit the Little Pebble Bar in the late afternoon and drink until it got towards sunset and then head out and fish all night, drinking beer to taper off." Many gillnetters made one set, hit the sack and didn't haul their net until morning. Not Ron and Knute. "We fished hard. Set the net, wait for an hour or so, pull her in and set again. Many a morning I cleared enough to pay my rent for two or three months."

Before he met Gloria and got married in the mid-seventies, Ronnie was a strenuously frolicsome drinker who, while maybe not actively looking for trouble, was cheerfully willing to settle with fisticuffs any arguments that might arise. There were lots of bars in Ballard and around Seattle where a good-looking, extremely confident guy like Ron could easily find himself in dispute over any number of things—women, sports, or the best way to bait a crab trap.

Which may explain one particularly large scar on his nose. "We were drinking one night at Ray's," he explained sheepishly, "and somebody bet me that I couldn't run at a stop sign on a 4x4 post and knock it over." He did, but it required a lot of facial repair work. "Actually I figure I broke my nose 11 times. First time when I was 13. Then fights and stuff, a couple of times playing racquet ball. This big scar on my temple is from the time I jumped off a truck doing forty coming back from the Fisherman's Bar up in Naknek. Only time I was knocked out. Didn't get the gravel out of my skull until the next year. Seven pieces. I used to think I was invincible."

His recreational enthusiasms aside, Ron maintained a firm grip on his fishing ambitions. "When the weather got good around April and May, most of my buddies would start talking about going to the beach. But me, I'd start thinking about Bristol Bay."

CHAPTER 4

"My Dad started coming with me to Bristol Bay in 1971 and he liked it a lot. He and I would fly up about ten days early to get my boat ready. We'd go to town every night and keep getting thrown out of places so by the end of the week we had to do our drinking down on the boat. We called it Norwegian Training Camp. My friend Walter Christiansen came with us in 1980. Last night before the opening we were drinking tequila and Dad was matching Walter and me shot for shot. He woke us up at dawn, hangovers and all, and served us fried eggs from a spoiled batch that he'd been saving. It was an old halibut boat trick. He always used to say, 'Let's see how brave you guys are in the morning.'"

To this day, Bristol Bay still has the largest annual salmon run anywhere on earth. About three hundred miles southwest of Anchorage, the vast open bay is the crook of the elbow formed by continental Alaska and the great Alaskan peninusla that swoops down to form the Aleutian chain.

Even though the land around the bay is well below the Arctic

Circle, it falls within the arctic climatic zone because it is wide open to the wintry blasts that sweep down across the Bering Sea. The flat, hummocky tundra is basically treeless except for balsam poplar, dwarf alders and willow thickets which grow down along the riverbanks, bogs and potholes. Here and there a few scraggly spruces—a ten footer is probably 30 years old. Shrubbery runs to bog blueberry, Labrador tea, crowberry, bearberry and mountain cranberry. From the air, the country is gorgeous with lovely subtle browns and greens traced by the aimless serpentine meanders of the creeks and the rivers. It's also stunningly beautiful if you get down on your hands and knees and peer closely at the intricate mat of grasses, mosses, lichens and tiny arctic flowers. But from eye level, the scene is as dull as Kansas except when it's clear enough to glimpse the mountains in the far distance.

The five major rivers* which feed the bay wind their way across the tundra from the big crystal clear lakes that provide God's own perfect spawning ground for all five species of Pacific salmon. But most specifically and spectacularly the Sockeye. The Bristol Bay Sockeye runs have been clocked as high as sixty million fish over a three to six week period starting in late June every year. They come in huge schools from the Gulf of Alaska below the Aleutians and can be seen from the air heading north through the passes along the island chain into the Bering Sea. By the time they near the river openings, the schools have become invisible in the silty waters of the shallow bay and give evidence of their presence only when they leap—a slashing, questing forward lunge toward their upstream destiny. After they enter the gin-clear rivers they again become visible, swimming in undulating skeins up to the one lake where they were born. By the time they arrive their backs are bright crimson.

---

* *Their jawbreaking names: Nushagak, Naknek, Egegik, Ugashik and Kvichak. Less important are the smaller Togiak, Igushic and Meshik Rivers and the curiously named Wood.*

The fish originally supported settlements of Aleuts, Eskimos and Athbascan tribes. The runs provided easy streamside fishing with spears, rudimentary traps and nets. As aboriginal subsistence went, it was rather pleasant living except for the bears, mosquitos and frostbite.

But because of the abundance of food, the natives had enough energy left over to indulge in a good deal of intertribal territorial warfare. (Further north, above the Arctic Circle, survival is so difficult—and life so precious—that the Eskimo language doesn't even contain a word for murder.)

Captain Cook came through the Bay in 1778 and noted, "We saw many leaping salmon in the sea and some were found in the maws of cod which we caught." The Russians were also well aware of the salmon, but were far too busy with fur to bother with them. Same with the Americans until 1882 when the schooner *Neptune* caught and salted the first commercial quantity of Bristol Bay salmon. The following year, the Arctic Pack Company built a cannery at Nushagak and produced 400 cases of salmon. In 1885, Alaska Packers of San Francisco established the first of its many canneries in the area. Several dozen large sailing ships from Seattle and San Francisco started coming north every summer with deckloads of sailing fishboats and big crews of fishermen, mostly Italians and Irish from the Bay Area and Norwegians and Yugoslavs from Puget Sound. Descendants of many of these early fishermen still return to Bristol Bay every year as surely as the Sockeye themselves.

Under the territorial stewardship of the United States Government, all Alaskan salmon runs eventually became seriously overfished, thanks to the unrelenting greed and political clout of the major fishing companies based in the lower 48, as well as the incursions of Russian and Japanese fishermen. But after statehood was granted in 1959, the fishery came under the management of Alaska's own biologists, fishermen and politicians and the salmon resource throughout the state gradually began to take a turn for the better. By 1973, five years after the state took over, the total Alaskan catch hit bottom at 22 million fish because of the depredations of foreign fleets still fishing up to the three mile limit off Alaskan coasts. But the Magnuson Act in 1977 extended the limit out to 200 miles and by 1982 the catch rebounded to more than 109 million fish with increases in all species. Today, virtually all the runs are in good shape, although unpredicted variations can be drastic and extremely dire for both the commercial and subsistence fishermen.

With five different species of Pacific salmon and dozens of districts and thousands of different streams in which the salmon spawn at widely varying times of the year, managing the Alaskan salmon resource presents a complicated challenge. The Bristol Bay Sockeye run is especially difficult for the state biologists to understand, predict and control.

To begin with, the hatchling Sockeye smolts may decide to spend from one to four years in their natal lakes before heading out to the sea. And when they get there, a given fish may achieve sexual maturity in from one to five years before heading back upriver to spawn. Getting a handle on these lifecycle variables is further complicated by climactic conditions. Extremely severe winters may kill the eggs where they lay in the gravel lake beds and streams thus diminishing the future runs. And oceanic weather cycles such as El Nino affect the location and abundance of feed. In the Sockeye's case that feed is primarily plankton. Unlike other species, the Sockeye have no teeth on their lower jaw and only vestigal teeth on the upper. While they will feed on krill and squid they don't eat herring. The returning fish usually weigh from four to six pounds and as they emerge live from the water their backs are a luminous greenish blue. Rich in oil, their flesh is delicious fresh, frozen or canned. Depending on where it feeds and where it spawns, the King salmon are the only specie even richer in oil than Sockeye. Recently, the Kings returning in April to the Copper River in the central Alaskan coast near Cordova have become highly prized and astronomically priced in trendy restaurants in the lower 48. But Alaskans know that in truth, the choicest King salmon of all are the big boys—and girls—

who come in from the sea to the mouth of Yukon River powerful and fat enough to travel up to 2300 miles before spawning. Almost all of these fish are reserved for resident subsistence fishermen.

Because the returning salmon can't see in the muddy waters of the Bay, they are caught in daylight using gillnets. The state now limits the fishery by carefully regulating the number of permitted boats and the length of the nets. The times allowed for the next day's fishing are announced on the radio based on the escapement counts of state biologists stationed on towers in the rivers upstream from the Bay.

Originally, Bristol Bay fishboats were cannery-owned, double-ended, 32-foot open wooden sailboats with a single mast. With two man crews, they would be towed out by company tugs in a long line of boats to the grounds. Nets were hauled by hand, salmon delivered to anchored tenders. Built by the hundreds down south and brought up on the ships and left on the shore every winter, the boats were crude and murderously dangerous in the sudden summer storms that rake the fishing grounds. The tidal range in Bristol Bay frequently approaches 30 feet. Add river current to the current of outgoing tide directly against a Bristol Bay gale and you have a recipe for *extremely* rough water. No wonder one of the major tidal mud flats is named Dead Man's Sands. In 1953 the state of Alaska mandated that in the interests of safety, Bristol Bay fishboats could be powered, but their length still could not exceed 32 feet. And that's the rule to this day.

How that 32-foot limit has evolved over the past 50 years is dramatic testimony to man's maritime ingenuity. The first Bristol Bay powerboats were trim little vessels with a small forward cabin with a couple of berths, head and galley. Although many of these boats still are still fishing, today's most modish designs are big, boxy, V-bottomed aluminum jobs—high, wide and ugly with bobbed-off noses to stay under the 32-foot limit. But they have huge capacity relative to their length and most now have powered net reels and compartmented chill tanks that keep the fish fresh in 32-degree sea water. These aluminum boats are designed to work the shoals around the river mouths and take groundings without damage. Beamy and shallow, they pound and have an abrupt and jarring motion in the waves. And being aluminum, they're noisy. But they can't be beat for durability and functionality. They're hauled out on shore and sit out in the weather on blocks during the fall, winter and spring, and except for nets, engines and equipment they require very little maintenance. The only paint they need is the name on the bow and permit numbers on cabin side.

Ron's first Bristol Bay boat was fiberglass. And although the Sockeye runs were scanty in the early '70's—there was no opening at all in 1973—he fished hard and managed to survive. But what turned out to be more important than how many fish he caught in those early years was his success in angling for permits. Because 1970 was a qualification year, he received a permit in 1974 for free. The next year he bought another permit for $1000 and put it in his Dad's name. And then in 1976, to the amazement of most—and the chagrin of very many—the citizens of Alaska voted Limited Entry for the entire Alaskan salmon fishery—fewer boats and only with a specific area and specie permit. Thus Ron's two Bristol Bay permits and his Southeast permit suddenly became worth real money.

About the same time, a new fishery boom began in Alaska with Alaskan King crab. It started around Kodiak Island on the south side of the Alaskan Peninsula. But the discovery of huge shoals of these giant crab in the Bering Sea set off a maritime gold rush. The greatest concentrations of the King crab were offshore, far beyond the three mile limit and thus outside the state's Limited Entry control. That made it a case of devil take the hindmost. Young Ron Peterson's sharp instinct for opportunity turned unerringly to crab.

CHAPTER 5

The weather over the Bering Sea is generally bad
and very changeable. Good weather is the exception and
does not last long when it does occur.
—United States Coast Pilot, Volume 9

These two laconic sentences sum up one of the worst climates on earth. In the summer, gales may cheerfully blow from any direction, but in the winter hurricane force storms with winds as high as 125 miles per hour come screaming out of the Northwest across the top of the world above Siberia. Seas become mountainous, and the blowing spray freezes instantly on the rigging of any ship or fishboat. (One inch wire cable exposed to the wind will ice-up to a diameter of over one foot!) And winter, of course, is crab season on the Bering Sea, when the shells are hard and the meat is prime. If you doubt that certain men still willingly take amazing risks to make a buck, shake the horny hand of an Alaskan crab fisherman. And if you'd enjoy dining on something that somebody put his life on the line to catch, order the Alaska King crab.

What you'll be eating is *Paralithodes camtschaticus,* red King crab, the largest of the 71 species of crab known to exist in Alaskan waters. The biggest male on record weighed 24 pounds with a wingspan of nearly five feet. The red King species is found from British Columbia to Japan with the largest concentrations in Siberian waters, the Kodiak archipelego and the eastern Bering Sea off Bristol Bay. Closely related species are the blue King crab and the brown King crab. In Alaska, the blues are mainly found between the Pribilov Islands and St. Mathews Island in the central Bering Sea. The brown Kings are deep water crab and make their home in the subterranean canyons further west out along the Aleutian Chain. All turn red when cooked, all are sold as Alaskan King crab, and all are equally delicious.

Crabs are mysterious creatures. Just as geologists have learned so much of what they know from what is revealed by road cuts, marine biologists wisely follow commercial fishermen around to extend their knowledge of what's actually down there below the surface of the sea. All agree that much remains to be known about crabs. My friend Ronnie thinks there are big crab everywhere, off all continental shelves around the entire globe. Large quantities of the red King crab have recently been discovered off the coast of Norway. Australians dine royally on totally different species of big crabs found at various points around their continent., but none of the Australian crabs is as large as the kings.

Like all crabs, the King crab will eat just about anything, starting with plant and animal plankton when they are mere swimming larvae just out of the egg. Then as they mature their diet includes starfish, worms, clams, mussels, snails, sea urchins, sand dollars, barnacles, fish parts and each other. And in turn, many marine creatures make a meal off them including (but not limited to) octopi, sculpins, halibut, cod, and sea otters. Man, of course, is another mighty predator and besides the ones we keep for ourselves, the undersized and female crab tossed overboard from a crab boat are easy pickings for hungry codfish as they slowly sink down the water column to the bottom.

As befits such long-legged creatures, the adult red and blue

King crabs cover a lot of ground. (The deep water brown crab do their migrating vertically—up and down their submarine mountains.) Annual migrations of the reds and blues cover 100 miles or more from deep water to the shallows where they mate and molt in the spring before heading back to deeper water in their offshore feeding migration. On the way, the younger crab of both sexes will occasionally form huge piles or "pods"—whether for fun or protection it's hard to say. In any case, for the crabbers, the trick is to find the migrating mature crab and stay in front of the "herd" as it moves. Their brains are minute and what goes on in the tiny mind of a crab is anybody's guess. They have eyes to see, but they are guided more by smell than sight. They are lured into the pots by the tantalizing scent of chopped herring in the bait containers.

The King crab fishery actually got off to a rather slow start. The Japanese and Russians had been catching and canning King crab since the 1890's and until World War II, several million pounds a year were exported to the U.S. And a few local fishermen out of Kodiak Island had also dabbled with catching and canning the local King crab before the war. After the war, exploratory attempts to commercialize the King crab fishery grew slowly and spasmodically, with the fishing confined to the south side of the Alaskan Peninsula. By the 1950's fishermen had discovered the crab concentrations in the Bering sea and by 1953 the catch had grown to 4.5 million pounds with much of it frozen as well as canned.

The early King crab fleet was a very mixed bag—most of the boats were under 60 feet and included converted salmon seiners, trawlers, tenders and sardine boats. Many of these boats—as well as their gear and their crews—were not equal to conditions they had to face. It soon became apparent that loss of life, limb and vessels in the crab boat fleet was going to be higher than in any other fishery in Alaska. Since the first caveman with a net venturered forth on a couple of logs tied together with vines, the design of fishing boats has been a matter of trial and error in a specific body of water at a specific time of year—what works, what doesn't work, what sinks, what floats. The Bering Sea in winter was a particularly stern and unforgiving proving ground.

But despite the risk, the rush was on. The crab were there and specialized boats and gear were being evolved to catch them.

Big crabs, of course, mandated big pots. After much experimentation, the design evolved into big steel-framed box traps up to eight feet square and three feet deep and weighing as much as 800 pounds empty and a ton or more when full of angry and frustrated crab. Handling big pots took big gear. A powerful deck crane was needed to pick each empty pot off the stack on deck and place it on a hydraulic platform that tilts up to slide the pot over the side into the water. Individually buoyed, the pots were set in long strings, allowed to soak for from 12 hours to several days before being retrieved. When hauled in, each pot was again set on the pot launcher, the door opened and the crab allowed to slide out on deck where crewmen quickly throw the females and undersize crab overboard and slid the males into the holding tank where circulating fresh seawater to keeps them alive and in good condition. Owing to the constant motion of the boat at sea, the crab in the live tanks can eventually chafe against each other so much that their shells are fatally abraded despite their spiny thickness. This puts a constraint on how long a crabber can stay at sea before heading to port to transfer the still living crab to a processor. (No money for dead crab.)

All this happens, of course, in a frantically short season, under extreme sea and temperature conditions. The hazards are several. First off, the crab boat heads out to the grounds with a large deck load of very heavy pots which raises the boat's center of gravity dangerously. Well designed boats not properly ballasted with fuel and water have been known to roll over even in conditions that were relatively mild by Bering Sea standards. But even a properly ballasted crabber with a full deck load of pots may be caught by blowing snow and spray which turns each of its pots into an extremely heavy cube of ice. Again, often with fatal consequences. Trying to tarp off the deck load under icing conditions is a life or death exercise. It has been done. But not always in time.

But let's say the crabber gets out to the grounds, successfully launches the pots, lets them soak for a day or two and is ready to haul. It now starts to blow a full gale, or even more, a hurricane with winds up to 100 miles an hour or more. No Bering Sea crabber can be surprised. The recourse is to "jog" into it until the wind abates to a reasonable 40 or 50 knots. Go back and try to find the pots. Maybe it has turned cold enough for advancing winter sheet ice to shear off the buoys. But say there was no ice, say they found the pots OK and pulled them. No crab. *Shit!* Do it all over again and hope for better luck the next haul.

A few days later maybe it's blowing hard and cold enough for the boat to start to ice up. The crew has to turn to with axes and baseball bats to break the ice off the superstructure to keep the vessel from getting top heavy and rolling over. That done—successfully this time—the pots are hauled again. Plenty of crab. "We're on 'em now!" Keep fishing, keep hauling, keep sorting. No time to sleep. One guy at a time rotates for six hours rest. Everybody else on deck, 24, 30 or 36 hours at a time. The work is backbreakingly hard, difficult, dangerous. Working in a trance. So many ways to get hurt—slip, fall, caught, crushed, maimed. Or even overboard. I used to have a drink occasionally with a couple of guys named Tor and Sigmond at Ray's Boathouse. Sig got knocked into the sea one time by a swinging pot and Tor gained a measure of Ballard fame by immediately diving overboard to save him, an act that could easily have cost him his own life in the fatally cold sea.

As the sixties became the seventies, the boats kept getting bigger and stronger with gear to match. But the crab were still crab, the sea still the sea, and fishermen still mere mortals.

CHAPTER 6

"The first King crab boat I crewed on was the old
Valiant *in '73. It was exciting and big money and I wanted*
to get in on it. You could get Marco to build you a crab
boat back then for three or four hundred thousand, but as
they caught crab, the price kept going up. It was like a
dog chasing a weiner on the end of a stick. The Marco
108-footers finally got up to a million, the 123-footers up
to two point two. And finally I just put a ten grand deposit
down on a big one and got on the list and figured, what
the hell, I'd find the rest of the dough somehow."

W hen he went on the hook for his crab boat, Ronnie was
all of 28 years old. But he was married by then and in addition to
a well-established reputation for thirst, he had made a name for
himself as a hard worker, a hell of a good fisherman and an
ambitious young fellow who kept his word and paid his bills—all
very valuable assets in the handshake-deal culture of the fishing
business. By 1978, he had been able to swing the purchase of
two new aluminum Bristol Bay boats thanks to the financial
intercession of a Ballard banker by the name of Floyd Unger. But

trying to round up the money for a Marco crab boat was another order of financial magnitude. Unsurpassed sea boats, the Marco crabbers were the Cadillacs—the biggest, the best-built, the most trouble-free and the most expensive. More than 100 of them were eventually built, and to this day none has been lost except for one hapless vessel that was steered on the rocks by a sleeping helmsman in narrow Grenville Channel south of Prince Rupert, British Columbia. (It was later raised and salvaged.)

The name "Marco" sounds Italian, but it's the trade name abbreviation of the Marine Design and Construction Shipyard down the street from Fisherman's Terminal on Salmon Bay. The company's guiding genius and sole owner is Peter Schmidt, the scion of a pioneer Washington state brewing family of pure German extraction. If you're from the West Coast and over the age of 40 you probably remember Olympia Beer. Peter was the Schmidt son who was too stiff-necked and proud to join the family business. He studied engineering, started his own shipyard and made a great success of it. Schmidt was an excelllent sailor. I used to race my own Cal 40 sloop against Peter's *Olympian* and he was a skillful and implacable competitor. While he could easily afford a much larger and more modern boat he still sails his original '60's vintage Cal 40—beautifully maintained, of course, at the Marco yard. His son, Hans, grew up crewing for Peter on the *Olympian.* Then while still in college, Hans bought his own Marco aluminum gillnetter and fished Bristol Bay. Now he's the manager of Marco's yard in Santiago, Chile, building huge and rakish 250-foot southern ocean tuna boats. Interesting men. Stubborn about quality.

Financing the *Aleutian Number One* was a scuffle.

"To start out with, there were three of us as partners—me, Nels Sorvik and Walter Christiansen—but when Walter dropped out, Nels and I still had to come up with six hundred and twenty five thousand cash before the boat was launched. I went around for about two years applying to the banks and it got to the point where I had gone to Peoples Bank four times in little over one year and the last time I went in, the guy I talked to wanted to start at the beginning and know everything about me. And I told him, 'Wait a minute, I been here four times and you're the fourth banker I've talked to, so let me hear a little history on you."

Exasperated, Ron again turned once more to Floyd Unger, the banker in Ballard. "Everybody kept turning me down, Floyd included, until we finally got it right, not borrowing too much, not counting on too much crab and having an alternative source of income, which in my case was Bristol Bay, and getting another partner—with money.

"Finally one day Floyd called me and said he'd had a guy come in the bank, a doctor, who was inquiring if he knew any young aggressive guy who wants to get into crab fishing. It was Dr. Frank Crealock in Ballard. So Floyd fixed me up with an appointment and I went over to his office and I talked to him for ten minutes and shook his hand and a couple of days later he called me and said he wanted to go in." An obstetrician who delivered more than 15,000 Seattle babies before he retired, Crealock was a man who knew a thing or two about humankind. "Doc Crealock told me later, 'When you walked in there and shook my hand and looked me straight in the eye, I knew it would work.'"

So Ron sold one of his Bristol Bay permits for $75,000 (the one he'd got for free), the second one for $45,000 (the permit for which he had paid $1000), one of his Bristol Bay boats for $80,000, emptied out his bank accounts and was on deck for the *Aleutian Number One,* slated for launching in 1981.

"A few guys slipped off the list, so finally our delivery date got moved up to September 22 of 1980, then up to September 22 of 1979 and they started building our boat. We were having great fishing in Bristol Bay in '79 but I realized that if we didn't get the boat until late September we were going to lose the whole King crab season for the year. So I called Al Engle, the yard boss at Marco, and I said, 'Al, what can you do to get this boat a month earlier?' And he tells me to call him back tomorrow which I did. Al said, 'If you come down and give me forty-five thousand cash, I'll do my best, no contract, no guarantees.' So I flew right back to Seattle. My partners didn't want to take the chance, but I put up the forty-five grand myself. The day I gave Marco the money there were about 20 guys working on the A-1. But two or three days later there was only one guy on our boat, a black guy and he was just sweeping. They'd put everybody on the two boats ahead of us to get them done. And I went a little nuts. But sure enough, the *Aleutian Number One* was christened on August 25th and I don't know how they did it because the night before, they were still putting formica down in the galley and like that. But they made it, a month earlier like Al said.

"So then we got the boat ready as fast as we could—pots, fuel, supplies, sea trials—and when we're all set to shove off, the damn railroad bridge outside the locks broke down and we couldn't get out of Salmon Bay. We were going crazy—all this money, all this effort, everything ready to go and we couldn't even get out of the locks. Finally three days later they raised the bridge for one hour and got it through.

"By the time the A-1 made it to Dutch Harbor the other crab boats were already coming in from their first trip, so Nels found out where the crab were. So we were able to salvage most of the two-month season and my partners paid me back their share of the forty-five grand. If the boat hadn't got up there in time, I think we'd have gone broke before we even got started."

But in truth the real trouble was just beginning.

Ron's partner, Nels Sorvik, was an experienced crab fisherman. But moody. He began to nurse a grudge because Ron hadn't accompanied the boat on its trip north to Dutch Harbor. Gloria Peterson had unexpectedly gone into labor just before the boat was leaving Seattle and Ron had given his word that he would be at her side when their first child was born. This rankled Sorvik. "Nels decided that he didn't want me on the boat with him at all."

Two and a half months later, with the season still going on, Sorvik steamed the A-1 all the way back to Seattle, tied it up to the dock and went home. "He hadn't even told me he was coming back and I didn't know what to tell Floyd. I mean, the season is still going on, we've got this big, beautiful, expensive boat, we owe all this money and it's sitting at the dock in Ballard. It was nuts."

The next year, 1980, proved to be the biggest King crab season in history—over 140 million pounds. A mature King crab weighs up to six pounds, and at over three dollars a pound, the A-1 should have made a killing. But again the boat missed half the season because the crew quit when Sorvik hired an extra man he had promised a job to in a bar. "This guy told Nels, 'You'd better take me or I'll sue ya.' So Nels did and the crew quit." More hard feelings port and starboard, fore and aft throughout the enterprise between partners, families, crew and lenders.

Then in 1981, the same thing happened again—the crew bailed out on Sorvik while the season still had a month to go. Ron went up and helped bring the boat back. "When we got home and tied up, Nels took the keys out and threw them at me and said he didn't want to have nothing to do with this boat anymore. And I went 'Oh.' He got so worried about the debt I think he just freaked out."

At this point Ron had to find another skipper. The man he found, Jostein Carlson, proved to be a gem and is Ron's partner to this day. Trained as an engineer, Carlson had been working as a machinist in a furniture factory in Norway, but fishing was in his blood. Like a moth to a flame, word of the King crab bonanza attracted him to Alaska in 1978 and he crewed on the famous crabber, *Alice B*, which in 1979 set the record of over a million pounds in a single trip. In Jostein, Ron had a man who was a dab hand with machinery, knew how to crew a crabboat and, thanks to his Norwegian genes, was an indomitable seaman.

So the 1982 season started with high hopes. Ron went up to Dutch Harbor in early September to work the deck and be the engineer with Jostein as skipper.

"We went out the night of the sixth and didn't get very far before the auxilliary engine blew. It was just poor maintenance, so we went back in and got it fixed and went out again. Half an hour later the whole main engine seized up and we barely limped in. We found out that Caterpillar [the engine manufacturer] had told Nels that we had some bad valve guides and it was a factory defect, just bring it in and we'll fix it and Nels never did. It caused so much blowby in the crankcase that the dipstick would almost pop out. The bad valve guides had caused carboning and scored the crankshaft and we were down for the whole season this time. And it was the first four-dollar King crab in history and one of the biggest seasons. And then we found out that the insurance we had placed on the first of September was no good, the company went bankrupt. We bought new insurance eight days later and then, by God, they went broke. Two in one year. We lost about sixty grand on our insurance plus our whole crab season."

Still financially afloat, but gasping for breath, Ron and Jostein took the boat north again in the fall of '83. This time they brought Floyd Unger along for the first trip to the grounds. "Floyd was the banker who was going to help us get out of our jam, So we wanted to show him how great the fishing was. And I had always told Floyd that you've never tasted anything better than fresh caught King crab. And we set out all our gear and we never even caught *one!* I finally ended up cooking him a codfish that we caught on the third day." The Bering Sea King crab fishery had gone from a high of 140 million pounds in 1980 to zero, zilch, nada in just three years.

Certainly the resource had been seriously overfished while under the regulation of the Federal National Marine Fisheries Commission whose policy can be most charitably be termed benign neglect. And to make things worse, the Bering Sea Pot Sanctuary—the crab spawning grounds—were also opened to bottomfish draggers during spring and summer and the bottom dragging undoubtedly had a serious impact on the crab population during the time when the crab were reproducing.

In fishing circles the argument about the effect of bottom dragging is a bit like the controversy about whether or not cigarettes cause cancer. But the dispute actually goes back to the Middle Ages. In the year 1366, the following petition was brought before the English House of Commons:

> "*Some fishermen who have during the past seven years by a new craftily contrived kind of instrument which amoung themselves is called Wondrychoun [apparently from the Dutch wonderkuil, "marvelous fishing trawl"], made in the form of a drag for oysters, which is of unusual length: to which instrument is attached a net so small a mesh that no kind of fish, however small that enters can pass out, but is forced to remain within it and be taken. And besides this, the great and long iron of the Wondrychoun presses so hard on the ground when fishing that it destroys the living slime and the plants growing on the bottom under the water and also the spat of oysters, mussels and of other fish, by which the larger fish are accustomed to live and be nourished.*"

The Dutch themselves didn't ban trawling until 1583, and in the following year, the French made fishing with a trawl a capital offense. By 1631 trawling was still in dispute in England when a trawl was described to the Privy Council as "*. . . a net . . . so as it sweepeth at the fish which lie upon the ground, great and small and bringeth the very sand up with the net: there is nothing that can 'scape*". The use of trawls was duly banned and the Royal Navy was directed to burn any trawl nets they might find aboard fishing vessels. Bottom draggers, of course, have historically maintained that the stirring up of the seabed has a salutary and stimulating effect on the biomass and they stoutly so argue down to the present day. In certain waters for certain species—hard shell clams off New Bedford for example—that may be true. But if you're in the market for a punch in the nose, walk into any Ballard tavern and loudly announce yourself for either side of the question.

Ronnie, of course, believes the draggers obviously do damage. "They went in the breeding grounds and it's like dragging a huge plow right over everything. Forty or fifty boats making four or five mile tows and making six or seven tows a day and sometimes they tow all night. And they were catching and destroying millions and millions of small crab."

Regardless of what caused the crash, *Aleutian Number One* was in big trouble. And it had plenty of company. In the winter of '83, after the empty-handed crab fleet limped back home to Seattle and tied up to Fishermans' Terminal, the joke going around Ballard was that you got a crab boat instead of a toaster if you opened an account at Seattle First National Bank.

Not only was the A-1 partnership on its last legs financially, the boat itself had gone from brand new to sadly bedraggled in just three years and needed repairs from stem to stern. Floyd Unger managed to find enough cash to keep them afloat. "Floyd got us a government National Marine Fisheries loan guarantee at a fixed rate when most of those boats were tied into one and a half or two over prime, which just broke a lot of guys."

With this enterprise-saving cash transfusion, Ron and Jostein found a good shipwright/mechanic and put him to work on the boat to bring it back up to snuff. "In two or three years, you can really take a boat down. It was a mess. We made a list of all the things that were wrong and we paid him $1200 a week which was good money for him and he spent about five months fixing everything right down to new washers in the faucets."

Once again the A-1 went back north. "I was just a kid with this beautiful boat and this beautiful big payment and I was just too dumb and ignorant and naive to think that we wouldn't go broke. I thought if we worked hard, we'd keep it. We did survey charter work, tagging crabs and pot fishing for cod every chance we could. And we cut down expenses, got rid of the fancy cars and basically told the bank that they were going to get every dime we didn't use for food, clothing, housing and the kids. We convinced them to hang with us, that eventually it was going to turn and they were going to get every cent we didn't need to live, and that's the way it was."

But it wasn't easy. "It was like a nightmare and it just wouldn't end. My wife kept saying, 'I'm tired of this boat, I want us out of it.' But I had a good partner in Jostein and we just kept going out and doing the best we could with whatever we could get. And thank God that Bristol Bay was pretty good those years."

Their salvation turned out to be the Opilio crab, better know to American housewives as snowcrab. Smaller and skinnier than King crab, they were also far more abundant—an untouched resource. "It was probably the end of '84, and we were only getting 30 cents a pound, but we started catching them in volume. Jostein got on to how to fish them and from November '84 straight through to September of '85 we had 3.6 million pounds at 30 cents and it was kind of the turning point."

But their troubles weren't over yet.

Doctor Crealock—along with a group of other medical men of his acquaintance—had become involved in the great investment-credit tax-writeoff dodge. They invested in new Gulf Coast oil platform supply boats and leased them back to the oil companies. The eventual popping of that bubble put Crealock and his friends in even worse shape than Ron Peterson. Dr. Crealock was under water up to the ten million dollar mark, but managed to get out of it without declaring personal bankruptcy which would also have sunk the Aleutian Number One as surely as a navy torpedo.

At the same time, Nels Sorvik, who was still on the books as part owner of the A-1, was also getting ready to file for personal bankruptcy. Something had to give.

"Floyd is with me and we're down at Rainier Bank and two guys in special credit came in to talk to us, guys I'd never met. And they told us that they had decided that they were going to be our thirty-percent partners. And I blew up. I mean by this time we were getting close to making the payment, you know, seventy-five or eighty-percent of what we owed. We had a tight budget that we were sticking to and times were lean and when they said they wanted to be a thirty-percent partner I just exploded. I told them, 'What the hell are you going to do—run the boat? You're too fat to work on deck!' I don't remember everything I said, but I told them to go ahead and take the whole damn boat and walked out. When I got home, Gloria asked me how did it go at the bank, and I said, 'Honey, I think I lost my temper.' And she said, "If you lost your temper, I know it's bad.

"I'm sitting in my basement that night talking it over with my Dad and I got a call from the attorney at the Rainier Interbay Branch and he told me on the QT that the next time the A-1 was in Dutch Harbor, the bank was going to tie it up and sticker it for a marshal's sale. And then a little later I got another call from Jostein in Dutch and he had just come in from a pretty good trip and he was all happy and I told him, 'That's just great, now get fuel as quick as you can and get back to sea.' I didn't have the heart to tell him that the bank was going to take the boat back.

"So I called Floyd later and said, 'Floyd, I really screwed up today, we've really got to do something.' And he met me early the next morning, five or six o'clock, and we went through this plan where we were going to go down there and apologize. And I did. I told them I'm sorry I blew up, but we've been struggling and we've done this and this and this and everything to make it a go. I've got a good skipper in Jostein and we're close to making it and if those other guys want out, let them out. You've got a better chance with me than with those other guys. I'm telling you, we're going to make it work. And you know, they went for it, gave us a five-year deal and Floyd got us new National Marine Fisheries financing about a year later and we paid Rainier off!"

Ron finally bought his partners out with a "cut and choose" deal. "I gave them their choice—they could buy me out for one dollar and assume my share of what was owed. Or I could buy them out for a buck apiece and keep the boat and take over all the debt. They had 45 days to reply." Dr. Crealock took a deep gulp, accepted Ron's dollar and remains his friend to this day. Sorvik was clearly in no shape to assume the debt and refused to even respond to the offer and remained Ron's embittered enemy until he died several years later.

As Floyd Unger told me one time, "After two or three deals with Ronnie, I just got kind of numb."

CHAPTER 7

*"Most business people sit down and crunch numbers
with a computer or a calculator trying to figure out the
bottom line. Ron just looks at a proposition and sees the
answer. He has a clear idea of the deal almost instantly. I
always say that if Ron Peterson was going through a
ghost town in the middle of the desert, he'd see something
that it would make sense to buy".*

—Floyd Unger

Floyd Unger had a ringside seat at most of Ron's deals, first
as his banker and eventually as his partner. Seriously Christian,
he's a guy of medium height, in his late fifties, round, but solid
with big hands and a handshake of impressive firmness. Cheerful
and good natured with an open-faced smile, Floyd flew the cold-
war Dewline between Wake Island and the Aleutians as a
radarman in the Navy. After that he started in the finance business
doing auto loans. Then he gravitated toward the fishing industry,
ending up in the Ballard branch of a major Seattle bank.

"Fishing is a scary business," says Floyd, "but all in all it's
better and less risky than contracting or restaurants. There's more

intrinsic value, and better people if you pick them right. Sure there are drunks and incompetents, but they don't last long. Even with the bad years, the fundamental value is there—the boat, the resource, the people. Good operators come out in the long run."

Fishboat deals: "It isn't the value of the boat. Over the years I've made a lot of guys mad at me over that. They say, 'How come you won't lend me a half million, the damn boat is worth three and a half!.' I always had to tell them that the loan is based on how much the boat can earn, plus what somebody is willing to pay for it today regardless of what it cost to build. But you take a fisherman who got enough money together to buy a big boat, go hire a crew, run the damn boat, find the fish and make a profit most years . . . that's a hell of a businessman as well as one hell of a tough human being. It takes a lot of guts to be a fisherman, and a lot of brains to be successful at it."

Floyd says Seattle is the only place in the world today that's both a fishing center and a money center for the fishing industry. Even with that, only the people who are actually in the industry understand it. The local gillnetters and trollers that sag forlornly at their slips at Fishermans' Terminal give the impression of an industry on the skids. That's true of the Puget Sound and Washington coastal fleets. But the long distance fishery—the seiners that go to Southeast every summer, the halibut boats and the long-distance crabbers and draggers and processors that go to the Aleutians and beyond—is thriving.

"People look at those beat-up, ice-scraped hulls of the fish boats and processors that come back to Salmon Bay and they think they're seeing an industry on the ropes. On the contrary. Even with all the ups and downs, this is still the busiest and most profitable era in North Pacific fishing. Those boats are worth a lot of money, and the owners are too. I'd have these guys come into me in their old clothes and put on the country boy act, and I'd say, cut it out, I know better."

That brings us back to Ronnie.

Ron says he grew up listening to his father go on and on

about how much money he could have made if he'd just bought Seattle real estate back when it was so cheap. "I decided I wasn't going to make the same mistake," says Ron. And whatever other missteps he may have made in his lifetime, being afraid to stick his neck out has not been one of them. And as Floyd Unger says, Ron definitely has a head for figures. He is amazingly quick about fish prices, quotas, insurance, and all the other fishing industry variables. His conversation runs along these lines: "I mean, what the hell, if I got even 12 guys in a Bristol Bay co-op and they averaged 35,000 pounds of Sockeye each and even if we didn't get any more than 55 cents a pound we'd still be grossing over $225,000." (Actually $231,000, but not bad while weaving a pickup through Ballard traffic.)

After narrowly avoiding financial disaster with the A-1 in the mid-'80's most sane individuals would have figured out that the simple act of going out crabbing in the Bering Sea in the winter would provide enough danger to slake one's appetite for risk. But Ron continued to tackle new problems, and to seek new opportunity.

The first problem he bit down on hard was trying to get the draggers off the Bering Sea crab grounds. To do that, he and some 60 other surviving crab boat owners got together to form the Alaska Crab Coalition and set about working to get the Bering Sea Pot Area put under State of Alaska rather than federal control. "That was a little bit like lying down with the devil, but it was better to have to argue with the state about limits and seasons than to try to do it long distance with the feds." The state cared more about the resource, and even though Alaska was—and still is—tough on the crabbers, the state waved the draggers off the field in 1987.

"Fishing politics is rough," says Ronnie, who was Coalition President for the first four years. "You've got to go up to Alaska on your own nickel and your own time and sit through days and days and sometimes weeks of testimony and hearings and you look around the room and most of the people there are paid lobbyists for the processing companies as well as other fishermen, draggers, seiners, gillnetters, crabbers, herring guys—everybody with their own axe to grind. And then you've got the politicians and the bankers the natives and the bureaucrats. It's wild and it takes it out of you. But that's what we had to do with the Crab Coalition.

"We had our own lobbyists at times. One time I went with the gal who was our lobbyist to visit the Governor in Juneau—I won't say which one—to drop off a five grand contribution to his campaign fund. I went on for about a half hour making my pitch on the need for state control of crabbing and after I got done and we were leaving he said, 'Well, that's fine, Ron, I got the message. But now what are we going to do about getting those damn Seattle crab boats out of the Bering Sea?' I kept my mouth shut for once."

Most of those surviving Seattle crab boats managed to stay afloat by adding dragging and trawling gear so they could also fish for pollock and sole. Ron decided to keep the A-1 as she was—a straight crabber—but had considerable success pot fishing for cod when the crab season was closed. The big 700-pound crab traps had one-way plastic fingers installed in the openings. The cod, attracted by cut herring in the bait basket, could swim in but not out.

So what with the Opilio and the research charters, the *Aleutian Number One* managed to hang on and start to make real money during the late '80's and early '90's. Which gave Ron time and energy for another wild idea.

This time he took on the Russians.

CHAPTER 8

"I was president of the Alaskan Crab Coalition and at that time we were fishing Opilio right up on the line from St. Matthew to the Aleutian chain that was supposed to separate our fishing area from the Russians. Depending on which way you interpreted the latitude and longitude, there was about a thirty-mile gray area and we were fishing in there and so were the Russians and they started chasing us around with gunboats."

Ron is an aggressive fisherman. If there's a line beyond which fishing is forbidden, he will fish right up to that line. Maybe on it. Well, hell, maybe once in a while a teensy bit over. That's how he fishes Bristol Bay, that's how he'll always do it wherever he drops pot, hook or net. Never mind that the fishing might actually be better far back from the line. If there's a line, he wants to be right up to it. Several years ago while struggling to set his gillnet during a gale at Egegik in Bristol Bay, the Alaska Fish and Game spotter plane turned him in for being over—a serious, license-losing offense. Ron got off with a slap on the wrist by convincing the authorities that because of the gusty 60-knot winds, the plane was bouncing all over the sky even worse than he was on the water and couldn't possibly have arrived at an accurate fix on his position. Ronnie and risk. Both begin with R. As does Russia.

After provoking and being provoked by Russian gunboats, Ron complained to the U.S. government and ended up getting involved with Ed Wolfe, a State Department lawyer specializing in fishing issues. Wolfe worked out an understanding with the Russians over the disputed area. This brought up some interesting possibilities.

Ron: "We realized that there was a thing called a "giffa"—a government international fishing agreement that meant that if they were allowed a fishery in our country, we should get one in theirs. So we started lobbying to fish crab over there in Russia."

The Russians, of course, had been fishing for King crab even longer than Americans. And Ron and the other American crabbers were sure that their resource had scarcely been touched. There was a line. It stood to reason that the fishing was better over on the other side—the Russian side. And in this case they were right. The Russians had plenty of crab, few boats, and no market.

In March of 1987, Ron accompanied a delegation of 14 fishermen to Siberia to try to work out a deal. "Everybody said it had been tried before and we'd never get a treaty, but that's exactly what we came home with, a signed treaty to fish crab in Russian waters and it was pretty damn neat."

Ron got along famously with the Russians. Two years earlier, back in 1985, he had participated in a "Citizens' Summit" TV program linking by satellite an American audience in Seattle with a Russian audience in Leningrad. Phil Donahue hosted the American side and Vladimir Posner the Russian. Ron was in the audience and became exasperated when Donahue kept throwing the Afghanistan issue at the Russians rather than engaging in what Ron thought was a meaningful dialogue.

"I was in the front row and was standing up to leave, and Donahue put his arm on my shoulder and asked me what was wrong. I told him 'You know, you really had a chance to do something here with these people and all you're going for is argument and ratings. I came here to talk with some Russian fisherman.' Well the Russians stood up and started cheering when they heard the translation. I was kind of ticked off but I sat down. And about thirty minutes later this guy in the Leningrad audience stood up and said that he was a famous Russian painter and he wanted to paint a picture of 'the fisherman with the fire in his eyes.' A year later I got a call from KING-TV and the Russian painter was here with a Soviet film crew to paint my picture. He did it down on the A-1 and I have it at home."

Negotiating the crab deal in Russia turned out to be instructive.

"When I went over there with the delegation the first time in '87, it was still Communist, so you knew there was some semblance of order, but no money. We'd go over there and wine and dine and entertain them, and when they came over here we'd wine and dine and entertain them and they'd say, 'Captain, this capitalism is the greatest thing ever created. Everything is free. You don't need any money to be a capitalist, just do business with a rich American.'"

The Russians had the crab but the Americans had the cash and the technology.

"They knew the *Aleutian Number One* over there because they had chased us around and took pictures of us. There it was with those big American flags painted on the bow. And they were flabbergasted because our boat with a crew of five got more crab than their 250-footers caught with a crew of 25. But we had better gear and a better way of fishing and our crews are on shares not straight monthly wages like the Russian guys who got paid no matter how much they caught. And they wanted to buy the A-1 and take it to Russia, but they wanted the crew and skipper to stay a year. They loved that boat. I've got a picture with the head Russian guy and the State Department guy all at my house along with KGB guys and the whole outfit."

But for once, Ron Peterson decided to pass.

"After what I saw over there and all the payola and stuff like that, I figured I'd be smart to drop out. You were supposed to do a joint venture with a Russian company that had access to a quota and you brought your American boat over and reflagged it Russian and did kind of a fifty-fifty split. The crab was sold in Japan or America and you split the money. Some guys made big money over there and the fishing was phenomenal. But you never knew who you were paying off. Everybody had their hand out, so you didn't know who was the right guys. It just seemed too complicated to me. Our fishing was good in the U.S. and I didn't want to take the boat to Russia and sell it and worry about losing it. The Russians were putting up almost no money, all they had was their quota. I was way too small to play that game and it wouldn't have been enjoyable."

Still, as Ron says, some have made big money over there helped significantly because of a loophole in the law—the Russian crab caught by American vessels was marketed as American crab thus avoiding the seven percent tariff. Low price and abundant supply eventually caused the U.S. price of crab to crash in the mid-'90's. The deal Ron had helped put through, ended up hurting the crabbers—like himself—who stayed on the American side of the line.

"Now it looks like they're finally running out. There's still boats over there fishing, but according to the people who are involved with it, the crab are getting smaller and smaller. They're getting down to two-and-a-half pounders when a normal mature male would be six pounds. On paper, it's actually pretty well regulated, but there's so much corruption and bribery that people were taking double and triple quotas. So it's amazing that it lasted for twelve years considering the amounts they were taking."

According to Sir Isaac Newton's first law of motion, a body continues in its state of rest unless it is compelled to change. Newton's law obviously doesn't account for the restless energy of Ron Peterson. After passing on the Russian deal, it didn't take him long to find another way to stick his neck out.

CHAPTER 9

"I've had about 19 or 20 boats, from 32 feet on up to
335 feet. Some of them I never even told my wife about."

When it comes to compensation, fishermen and farmers are at the wrong end of the food chain. They do the work to catch or grow the food, run the biggest risk and get the smallest return. The boys down at the feed store call that sucking hind tit. Naturally, the food processors, food brokers, food company executives and food retailers will all go on and on about how tough their business is. Maybe so, but the guys behind the desks don't get bad backs and blisters, lose fingers, limbs—or lives—putting on their 100% markups every step along the line. For fishermen and farmers the only sure payoff is plenty of fresh air and scenery. (In May of 2001, fresh Copper River Sockeye was selling in Seattle grocery stores for $8.99 a pound. The buyers in Cordova were paying an even buck.)

Fishermen are especially vulnerable. There are no price supports on fish. And no guarantees about what the ocean might or might not yield. A big catch nearly always means low price. And while a small catch usually means higher price, not infrequently it's both small catch *and* low price. Take it or leave it. Eat your own fish and be damned.

For a guy like Ron Peterson, the temptation to get into processing was far too strong to resist. Get a bunch of guys together, form a co-op, go buy a processor and beat the system.

Traditionally, Alaskan fish has been processed by shore-based canneries. Big, heavy machinery. Steel cans. Lots of labor. But since World War II, more and more floating processors have entered the scene, nearly all of them based on frozen product instead of canned. It's a relatively easy proposition to refrigerate a ship's holds—spray on the foam insulation, install piping, add an extra diesel engine or two to power the compressors and you're pretty much set. And the processing crew stays on the boat and can't go to town to get drunk or thrown in jail. Fishermen transfer their catch to tenders which consolidate the catch from a number of boats When they are loaded, the tenders bring the fish to the nearby processor. The fish come on topside. Slime line is on a 'tween deck where the fish are cleaned and graded. Most salmon and halibut are frozen whole. Sole, cod and pollock are cut and packaged. Processors transfer frozen product in pallet loads of cardboard boxes to tramp steamers that take the catch to market— Japan or the U.S. for most Alaskan seafood. At the end of the season the floating processor either goes to a home port or moves along to the next opening. Slick.

Nowadays, there are big factory ship trawlers in the North Pacific that both catch and process huge quantities of pollock— a cod-like species that was considered worthless until the factory ships perfected the system of catching, cleaning, portioning, packaging and freezing the fish all within hours before they had a chance to go soft. Labels are slapped on later, by the ultimate marketer of the product—Mrs. Paul's for example.

The Alaskan floating processors are mainly big barges and converted World War II freighters, although the processing fleet now includes a ramshackle variety of other vessels, large and not so large.

"In 1989, I really wanted to get into processing so I put ninety thousand down on the *Ocean Pacific,* an old converted hundred-and-eighty-foot ex-U.S. Navy YW water tanker. The boat plus a barge were almost two and a half million and I had forty-five days to come up with the financing or I'd lose the ninety grand. So I got twenty-three real hot salmon fishermen from Bristol Bay and False Pass to come in on it and we put the deal together in time for the '89 season."

Ron had a friend who was managing another processor, the *Yardarm Knot,* when it ran on the rocks up in the Pribilofs the year before. He looked at Ron's *Ocean Pacific* deal, bought 15 percent of it and brought along about 70 of the best workers from the *Yardarm Knot's* processing crew.

"We left Seattle in May and got up to Togiak [up the coast from Bristol Bay] four hours after the opening and we processed five hundred tons of herring at five hundred bucks a ton for the next five days which was a quarter-million dollars. Then we went to False Pass and did nine hundred thousand pounds of Sockeye and then around two-point-six million pounds in Bristol Bay. We had a hell of a year! I mean that boat was making a lot of money. Then it went down to Southeast and it was a huge pink salmon year and the boat was processing a hundred fifty thousand pounds a day, seven days a week and things were going great. It was anchored three hundred yards from the Coast Guard dock in Tongass Narrows. One of the Western Pioneer trampers was tied up alongside taking fish, I think it was the *Bluefin,* and I'll be damned if they didn't manage to roll our boat over.

"It was a comedy of errors. The cargo started to shift and they couldn't get it shifted back in time and as more and more cargo slid, the list just kept getting worse. I'll never know why they didn't just run it on the beach or at least use the *Bluefin* to hold on to it. But they didn't. It took forty-five minutes for the *Ocean Pacific* to roll over and sink. I've got a videotape of the whole thing and it makes me sick to look at it. Flat calm, and all within three-hundred yards of the Coast Guard dock."

To make matters worse, Ron's friend, the manager—without

telling anybody—had opted to save money by dropping the hull insurance. There was other insurance, far less than the value of the enterprise, but just enough to keep the group together. Because the *Ocean Pacific*—before it sank—had been so profitable, Ron persuaded the members of the co-op to stay in the game and went down to Oakland and found the *Lock Knot,* a 335-foot surplus World War II freighter.

"Those old World War II Knot Ships make some of the best processor conversions. And the *Lock Knot* was the finest one in the world. It was babied. People lived on it and they had a professor that brought his classes aboard and worked on the engines and kept it spotless. It was cherry.

"We wanted to bring seven crab boats into our co-op and they were going to put up four hundred thousand dollars each, mostly CCF money—Capital Construction Fund—which is government loan money that you can use to buy new boats. We figured we could convert it for ten million and we were pretty sure of our numbers, but a lot of guys said it would cost at least twenty."

"The mistake we made was to give each salmon guy a vote and you never want to give fishermen a vote like that. At the end of the Bristol Bay season they had voted to pay themselves the highest price on their fish without having it sold to the broker. So it was all on borrowed money and that was a big mistake. So even though we had gone ahead and bought the *Lock Knot,* the guys voted against borrowing the dough to convert it. At that point, we could have traded it for another processor, the *Bristol Monarch,* which would have kept us going without maybe losing a season for the conversion. But then the guys voted no on that too. So when they didn't want to move, I said if you guys don't want to do something productive, if you just want to sit here and pay moorage, you better get yourself a new president. So another guy took over and they let it sit there for two more years paying four grand a month moorage plus insurance and finally sold it at a loss. I took a little hit on my share and that was the only time I ever lost money on a boat. Timing is everything and if we had done the knotship back then when Russia was getting involved we could have probably sold it to Russia for . . . . well, who knows."

Ron got one souvenir out of the deal—a small bronze plaque that reads:

> *"In appreciation of being President of Ocean Pacific Fisheries and having to wrestle in mud and spaghetti, we gratefully acknowlege your leadership."*

CHAPTER 10

"I'm convinced that the Mafia got legitimate and went into insurance."

Basically, a fishboat owner like Ron needs two kinds of coverage—hull insurance on the boat and liability on the crew. It was no big deal when Ron and his Dad with Walter Christianson along were fishing 32-footers in Bristol Bay. But when Ron got into a multi-million dollar Bering Sea crab boat with a crew of seven or eight, insurance got to be a very large number and an equally large headache.

Since then, he's really been to school on insurance.

His first expensive lesson came that time in 1982 when *Aleutian Number One's* engines failed. He had just bought a new hull and equipment policy, but when he submitted his claim he was chagrined to discover that the broker had placed the policy with a company that went bankrupt right after the premium had been paid. Sorry Charlie. No blood out of a stone. Dead out-of-pocket loss: fifty-thousand-some-odd bucks for engine repairs. The next insurance company he bought coverage from also went broke soon after—but in that case all he lost was the premium.

The lesson here is brutally simple. If a company suddenly has claims that exceed its ability to pay, it may politely tip its hat, go bankrupt and start all over again with a clean slate and a new name. Again: Sorry Charlie. And how does one know whether or not a company can or will suddenly be forced to go under? One does not. The carrier may have an excellent rating, but bad luck can sink it despite the best of intentions. This leads to the phenomenon of reinsurance: the primary carrier lays off a percentage of its risk—and its income—with other companies. In principle this is a sound proposition, again assuming reasonable luck and reasonable honesty all round.

Insurance companies, of course, have their own abundant store of horror stories about fraudulent claims. And Ron was an unwitting participant in a picturesque example. In 1983, one of his crewmen on the A1, a young Norwegian, complained of a sprained back. Refusing both Ron's offer of direct compensation for lost time and medical expense and the insurance company's subsequent offer of settlement, he sued Ron for four million dollars in a Seattle court. The case was tried before a judge who quickly developed an unusually intense sympathy for the handsome and blond young Nordic plaintiff. Things began looking expensive for Ron and his insurance company. But Ron had a cousin in Norway, a nurse, who lived near the village where the young man grew up. She looked up his records and discovered he had received a medical discharge from the Norwegian Army—bad back. Despite this new evidence, the judge promptly awarded $45,000 to the crewman. Upon threat of appeal, that was reduced to $30,000, but in a sudden spasm of fine print, the insurance company found reasons to deny responsibility. It took several more years of legal unpleasantness with the company, but Ron managed to recoup his attorney's fees and the award. The judge— for various reasons—later committed suicide.

Crab boat personal injury coverage became almost impossible to get in the early '80's when so many crewmen were being injured. "There was no limit on liability. A guy breaks his leg and the jury might give him three million bucks. There was no limit. So me and six other crab boats went to England. Lloyds of London wouldn't take us but they sent us on to one of the 'clubs' in the North of England.

"It was kind of neat," says Ron. "They were boat owners and they had managers and their own company. It was more blue water boats than fishing boats, but they had been around for one hundred and twenty five years and it was kind of a spin-off of Lloyds. So we went over there to meet them and they came over here and looked at us. They called us 'bloody Vikings' and we had a lot of banter back and forth about how we used to raid their shores a thousand years ago. But they let us in and it worked out OK, except that they had 'calls'. In other words, a personal injury claim might come up two or three years after the event and you'd have to pony up to pay the call. So you never knew where you stood from year to year or what your costs were going to end up being. But we had a hell of a record. At one point we represented two percent of the tonnage in the club and yet we were paying about twenty-five percent of the premiums. We were in there for about twelve years and we had a premium bank of about eight-hundred thousand of which they only had to pay out about eighteen thousand in our claims, so they got a lot of our money. We wanted a seat on the board and they kind of promised it but never gave it to us. And we didn't have a say, so we finally got out when American rates began to drop again. But they'd take us back any time. I learned a lot from the experience, I really did."

On one of his last trips to England, Ron was able to visit his father, Knute, in a hospital in Norway before he died. "We had a nice time."

On the A-1, Ron now pays approximately $6,000 per man per season for the first million dollars of personal injury coverage with a $10,000 deductible also out of Ron's pocket. A well-sprained ankle thus stands to cost him about $16,000, so he's more than willing to take care of minor medical expenses without submitting a claim. Fortunately, there have been no serious injuries—or claims—for over a decade and the A-1's safety record has kept premiums from going out of sight. Ron remembers paying only one major claim. The boat was up north of the Pribolovs and was coming back down after a very good trip. The crew had a case of beer and a bottle of vodka hid away and got to celebrating. No problems until next morning when one guy tried to wake up another one to go on watch. Hangovers. Fight. Broken door. Broken jaw. Finally got it settled. Insurance paid one third, Ron paid one third, guy who threw the punch paid one third. Everybody satisfied. Bring any more booze on the boat and you're fired.

For his hull insurance, Ronnie was finally able to get admitted to one of the Ballard private insurance pools. There are five of them covering various fleets—seiners, halibut boats, crabbers, trollers and gillnetters—all owned and run cooperatively by the boat owners themselves. The seiner pool alone covers more than 400 boats.

"I'm a director now, but I didn't get in the crab boat pool until 1985. They were leery about me because I've always been real aggressive and they saw that little bit of wildness in me. Plus we owed so much money on the A-1 that they were worried about us surviving. My mentors were guys like Karl Kuldestadt, Ole Hendricks and some of the other old-timers I looked up to. They taught me about a handshake and a word is your bond and we're all in this together as fishermen and you'd rather cut off your finger than have a claim. The guys all know each other and we know if somebody isn't taking care of his boat. Or somebody who starts drinking too much when he's running the boat. It's your money out there and you're betting on that guy fishing right alongside you, so you know. We have our own surveyors, the best, and we have requirements at haul-out. It's better than a Coast Guard inspection. We figure that hull insurance in our pool is about half of what it would cost on the open market. And we can trust it.

"The pools were started by Norwegian immigants and most of them didn't speak English too well and a lot of them never had that much schooling. But they were smart businessmen and they sat around and drank coffee and came up with a plan that has lasted 60-some years. They decided that if they couldn't afford boat insurance because it was so high, they'd figure out a way to do it themselves. Just basically collect enough money to take care of the boats in the pool. They each put up five percent of the value of their boat plus a promissory note for a thousand that was to be held for so many years. And what wasn't paid out in claims, they got back after four years. And they built these pools up from five or ten guys at ten thousand each until now we're talking about millions and millions of dollars. After the fifth year, you get the premium back from the first year and we've had one-hundred percent return from 1999 through 2001. We now have so much money in the pools covering so many boats that we have some of it in reinsurance, so the most we can lose is a four year premium. There was opposition to that from guys who said that we've been a going business for years and we've never been broke, but if you get a bunch of boats in a fire up in Dutch Harbor it could run thirty-five million easy. So the way we have it now, if we had a huge claim, the pool would pay the first half and the reinsurance the second."

Ronnie's cynicism about the insurance business runs pure and deep.

"Insurance is a funny thing when you start to break it down. There's a twenty percent commission on selling a policy. Add to that the cost of administration and you're up to sixty or seventy percent of your premium How much claims can you pay out of that?

"Reinsurance is even worse. You and I could sell it right out of this office. There's no course, no training, no certification. We could start right here. What we'd have to do is go to the Bahamas, you and I, or the Caymans, and sit in some bar down there for two or three weeks and kind of make ourselves known. And we'd buy into our own little company down there, then come back up and start taking millions of dollars worth of premiums written on our insurance company in the Caymans. And our records would be sealed from the Washington State Insurance Commission. So if we decided to default on a big claim, we'd probably lose our state license, but we'd still be able to keep all of our dough in the

Caymans. I mean, I hate to say that, but that's how rough some people play the game. You've got to be careful, real, real careful."

Despite his wariness, and insurance business scar tissue, Ronnie, like any other fisherman, can still find himself unpleasantly surprised by an insurance scam. His recent experience with the *Akutan* is a case in point. What happened is this:

Always on the lookout for another chance to get into processing, in 1998 Ron discovered a sistership to his old *Ocean Pacific* that was coming up for sale in a bankruptcy. Named the *Akutan*, it had seen service as a salmon processor in the Bering Sea. And although it was down at the heels and needed a lot of work, Ron planned to bring the boat up to snuff and add additional processing gear to handle both Bristol Bay salmon and crab during those seasons, then catch and process cod in between. At $1,500,000, he was the successful bidder and brought the boat down to Seattle and put it in the yard at Marco for repairs. (He also bought a cod permit to use with the boat, but the title to the permit turned out to be a tangled web that took three years to unsnarl.)

After hull repairs, the *Akutan* was relaunched and was just arriving under its own power at another yard for processing gear, when an ammonia tank in the refrigeration system blew out, forcing evacuation of the ship and the yard. Clean-up was a major job and it was discovered that ingested ammonia had caused severe damage to all five engines on board—two big main engines and three diesel auxiliaries that ran refrigeration, electrical and hydraulic systems.

Ron called the insurance broker. (The *Akutan* was not yet in a Ballard pool.)

The broker sends a guy down to the boat along with a surveyor and yes, by George, it's a mess and they promptly approve the claim for repairs. Ron goes ahead and authorizes the work with the trade—yard, engine companies and various other suppliers. The work is done, the bills come in to Ron. He sends them on to the company and gets a phone call. Sorry, Ron, it turns out that there's no insurance company. Turns out it's no longer in business. What about my premiums? Who's got that money? Well, gee, Ron, we're real sorry. Long story short: Ron is personally stuck with the bills. It runs about $250,000. Another mortgage on the house.

"Somebody's going to jail on that one and I'm not kidding. I mean I'm so mad because right now I've got to pay another twenty to fifty grand to an attorney to win my claim. But it's not about money any more. I want their scalp on the wall. A plaque and a newspaper article, so when people come in they can see that and remember . . . . *do not screw me!*"

You might be able to make it work on paper, but man-to-man, face-to-face, I'd say that cheating Ron Peterson is not a wise proposition.

CHAPTER 11

A lot of fishermen have died, but a lot of people get killed in other occupations too. If you want to go and risk your life, you can do it in any kind of work.
                                    —Jostein Carlson

Jostein fits fairly snugly in the classic mold of the taciturn Norwegian. (Ole and Sven go into a tavern to have a beer. When served, Ole looks at Sven and says, "Skoal". Sven's reply: "Did we come here to drink or talk?")

I dragged him out to my boat at Shilshole Bay one afternoon for a chat and it was like pulling teeth. He sat in the corner of the cockpit. "Want a coke?" "No I'm fine." "Make a pot of coffee?" "No thanks." "Want a beer?" "Too early."

I tried to get him going. "How rough does it get up there?" Answer: "If it gets too rough we just jog into it."

"Is it rougher than the North Atlantic?" Answer: "Depends on who's doing the bragging. I don't see that it makes much difference."

Carlson is in his early fifties, married, three kids, lives in Edmonds north of Seattle. He's about six feet, average build, sandy hair, tidy mustache. Talks to his wife twice a day over the radio when he's up north. Affably admits that fishing has been good for him, but hopes his kids don't go into it. "It's a gamble type of deal, you get it in your blood. It's basically what we do for a living. You take it or you get out."

I told him I was going to go over to Marco next week to talk to Bruce Whittemore the naval architect who designed the 123-foot crabbers like the *Aleutian Number One*. "Well, get ready for some bragging if you talk to Marco. They don't have a lock on the best boats, that's for sure. But not too many boats are any better." He should know. Over the past 25 years, the weather has culled the Bering Sea crab fleet remorselessly. In the winter of 2001 there were four hurricane force storms during the Opilio season in January. (In the Carribean, storms this violent would be individually named.) Seas crushed out all 18 pilot house windows of one 150-foot-crabber (Not a Marco boat.) The *Aleutian Number One* was first on the scene to render aid, but the damaged boat managed to stay afloat and was able to limp back down to Dutch Harbor.

It's certainly true that Marco is proud of its crab boats. Over 100 built and none of them lost at sea. Just the one that a sleepy helmsman ran on the rocks in British Columbia on the way north.

Ronnie, of course, is also especially proud of the A-1. "It's like a Viking ship of the twentieth century. Wonderful sea boat." But he also has a profound admiration for Jostein, the way he runs the boat, the way he runs the crew, the way he catches crab.

Ronnie says Jostein taught him a lot about how to handle the boat: Go easy. Take it slow. Don't jazz around at full throttle. If Jostein were a cowboy, he'd be the sort who is gentle on the reins. As skipper and part owner of the A-1, he watches it carefully, makes sure everything works, repairs what needs fixing immediately. Breakdowns cost money and/or fishing time. Worst case, a breakdown can also cost the vessel and the lives of the crew. (It's well to remember that thanks to gravity every airplane is trying to crash and all boats are trying to sink to the bottom and will readily do so given the first opportunity.) Since Ron's first partner and skipper almost destroyed the boat in its first three years of service, Jostein has run it for 20 years without a major breakdown. The vessel shows wear, but you'd never pick it out as a vessel with more than 20 winters in the Bering Sea.

The King crab fishery is famous being rough on crews. When they get "on the crab" many skippers still go around the clock and work the crew till they drop "Boogie till you puke" is not the style on the A-1.

"Jostein started our system in '85" says Ron, "Everybody gets six hours off every twenty four. So you get two fresh guys on deck every six hours. It makes a hell of a difference. If you know you're going to get six hours off, you know when you're going to eat. Two hot meals a day and snack all your want in between. So we go with Jostein and a relief skipper who also is the engineer, so he gets his six hours of bunk time with twelve in the pilot house and six on deck. Knock on wood. We have the best safety record in the fleet—never had a hull claim nor a major injury claim except for that one time. That's something I'm really proud of and it's due to Jostein and the way he runs the boat."

A number of A-1 crewmen have gone on to skipper their own boats. And that has much to do with how Ron chooses them and how he sends them forth. Ron: "I tell them it's OK to go up to town and all, but you have to learn to handle your money. You take a guy who doesn't want to go to college, wants to go fishing. Makes eighty or ninety thousand a year for ten months work. It's awful easy to waste it. I tell them how to save it, invest it. What the hell, even if you just put it in real estate you'll make something. Learn how to run the boat. Learn how to invest. I tell them how. We want to see them make it. After I hire a crewman, I sit him down in the office for a couple of hours and give him the lecture. They call it the Ron Peterson stare."

A new crewman on the A-1 only gets $100 a day for the first season. And that wage is actually paid by the other crewmen who split it between them and make sure they get their money's worth. If he makes good, the new guy is in for a full share the following year . . . if the crew votes him in.

It all works out. Eighteen hour days on a crab boat is obviously no walk in the park. But as Jostein points out, it's not constant work. The boat is moving between strings, waiting for pots to soak, running out from Dutch, running back. It's tough, but not a constant slam.

"That boat has changed a lot of people's lives for the better," says Ron. "We encourage the guys. We pay them top wage and they get good food. Any guy on a crab boat is bound to get a sprain or a bump once in a while, but for some reason Jostein and our guys don't put in the lawsuits they do on other boats. Some people, they sprain an ankle and they want to go home and sue you in the bargain. Our guys know they're paid pretty good and they've got a good job and they want to stick. We're more mom-and-pop than a big company and they've got my cell number and office number and they can call me anytime they want. We've been fortunate, we've got crew who've stayed with us seven, eight or nine years. And out of maybe two hundred and fifty crab boats in the fleet, about twenty of them are skippered by guys who started out on the A-1."

The big trick with the A-1 has been trying to stay in the game. When the red King crab crashed in the early '80's, Ronnie kept the enterprise afloat with his "odd jobs"—some pot fishing for cod, but mostly those research charters, tagging crab. Then it was the Opilio that really saved their bacon. In the '90's, the Opilio began to peter out and the red and blue Kings were coming back somewhat but with very short seasons. (One year, '92, no seasons at all.) It was the old story: too many boats, too few crab. For a couple of years, Ron made some money managing another crab boat, the *Dominator,* for a young aggressive comer named Chuck Bundrant. Constant scheming, planning, playing permit politics and trying to find an edge. Still and all, times were good. Between Bristol Bay and crabbing, the Petersons were doing very well.

Finally in '95, Ronnie took another big plunge. He borrowed another million bucks to modify the A-1 and the gear to go after brown crab out along the Aleutian Chain.

"Everybody said we were crazy," says Ron.

To make the boat safer and drier when bucking into a sea, the forward gunwale was raised about two feet, which projected the forward line of the bow some three feet. It worked. And by making the boat three feet longer, under the state Opilio regulations that put the A-1 in a larger class, allowing it to legally carry a maximum of 50 more pots—from 200 to 250. "We did it for safety, but guys stopped laughing and were really pissed when they found out we could carry more pots. I went from being the stupidest guy in Ballard to the greediest bastard."

But the major modifications had to do with going deep. Instead of red and blue King crab lying on flat seabottom from 50 to 100 fathoms, the brown King crab crawled on mountainous outcroppings down to 500 fathoms below the surface—so deep that even at an average depth of only 300 fathoms, a pot could take as long as eight minutes to hit the bottom. "It's like a bombing run."

Hauling from these depths required much more powerful retrieving gear—a big new hydraulic power block mounted on a reinforced deck plate backed by a 450-horsepower, eight-cylinder Cat diesel plumbed with two-inch, high-pressure stainless steel pipe. A new, more powerful crane was also needed—a "knuckle-boom" to pick the pots out of the water once they reach the surface.

And major modifications to handle much longer line.

Like most crabbers nowadays, the A-1 is rigged as a "long liner". Instead of an individual buoy for each pot, the pots are attached in a long string to a single line. On the A-1, the string consists of 75 pots each spaced 75 fathoms (450 feet) apart along the ground line. Allowing for the depth of line to the first pot, that means a ground line of one inch Spectra rope almost seven miles long! Brown crab pots are a little smaller—five-by-five-feet square and weigh about 300 pounds. Hauling them up from a maximum depth of 500 fathoms, the gear has to be strong enough to pull up a combined weight of up to 10 tons. The ground line itself has a rated breaking strength of 21,000 pounds, but pots can get caught and the line broken. Then Jostein and the crew must drag a 700-pound steel-pronged grapnel on a wire cable to snag the ground line again. So far no lost strings, although the first year they went after brown crab another boat intentionally set its string over the A-1's and cut their buoys. "We had a half-million bucks worth of gear on the bottom and if we hadn't found it, we'd have been out of business. It was a couple of other skippers were doing it, cutting other boat's lines and trying to screw them up. They accused each other and they ended up in court. Then a lot of dirty laundry got aired out and people went to jail. It's better now," says Ron, "because every boat now has to carry a full-time state observer who documents what you set and where you set it, so anybody who sets over you is going to get caught. They cost us three-hundred bucks a day plus their airfare to Dutch. Some of them are good, some are a pain in the ass, but in the long run, they're worth it."

Containing this amazing length of line on the deck of the A-1 required the construction of a line bin along the port side of the deck. An eight foot steel weather wall was built along the port rail, with a wooden wall ten feet inboard of that to contain the line. As the line comes aboard, a fairlead block sliding back and forth along a high rail automatically flakes the line down in the bin in 60-foot loops.

There's no pot limit on brown King crab, but the season is limited and only 17 boats have both the gear and the permits. The A-1 fishes up to 900 pots and goes out with some 10,000 pounds of frozen herring for bait. Carrying 300 pots per load, the A-1 must take three trips to get all the gear out. After the first 75 pots are baited and dropped, the crew launches the next 75, then the third and fourth. Then back to Dutch to get another load of pots and line. After all the pots have been dropped, the A-1 goes back to retrieve the first string which has then soaked long enough for most of the smaller crab to escape. "We use a large mesh so the little guys can get out and we soak long enough so almost all of the smalls can." The crab from each pot are sorted. The remaining smalls and females are thrown overboard and the keeper males dumped into the holding tank which is filled with constantly recirculating fresh seawater.

In the tanks, the crab remain fresh and alive, except, as previously noted, they will literally chafe to death in the sloshing holds if not brought in to port within several days—depending on how rough it has been.

Pots are rebaited as they are emptied—the new guy usually gets the job of filling the bait jugs and crawling inside the pots to rehang them from the top of the pot. The pots are then slid back aft and stacked in the stern. When all pots are again on board and ready to go, they are hooked up to the ground line and slide back into the sea one-by-one as the boat slowly moves along. Haul, pick, bait, dump, haul, pick, bait, dump until you've got a load or the crab shells are getting thin, then back to Dutch. Then back out to haul, pick, bait and dump some more. That's the way it goes for a brown King crab season lasting two or three months. Time out for bad weather doesn't count. It's is just time off the game clock which gives a second reason for crab fishermen to hate storms.

Jostein's secret weapon—although not so secret any longer—is a computerized three-dimensional bottom charting system which gives him an accurate visual representation of the rocky and precipitous contours of the bottom beneath the boat.

"I've had it since '88," says Jostein. "You need a fairly good computer. These days you should have a Pentium processor and some memory. You take the computer in and they'll customize it for you. You give them the charts of wherever you'll be operating and they digitize them for you. Everything will be on the hard drive. They call it vector scanning. It works on the contour lines. Everything is in proportion so you can blow them up and zoom in and out on the bottom and then you have the GPS hooked up, so it shows the boat as an icon on the chart.

"With brown crab, it all depends on how you haul the pots back in. You can rip them off if you haul up against the cliffs. You can tear the pots off and bust the lines and everything else.

You've got to be pulling away from the cliffs. Without the computer, I'd just be guessing."

The system is manufactured by the Electronic Chart Company of Seattle which was started by a local software engineer and a school teacher. It's now aboard some 500 or more vessels including tugs and yachts as well as fishboats of all kinds.

"I was the first one who got the program and I've been testing it for them since they started—actually before they went in business—and I've been doing that for quite a while now. I try to give them advice. Maybe they don't want to take it, but I try to use all the functions to make sure they really work, so I usually find out immediately whether something works or not, or if it crashed." The company is privately held, but the deal with Jostein gives him all the advancements and upgrades gratis as long as he fishes.

The latest wrinkle is a fully three-dimensional representation of the bottom that can be viewed from any angle with the position of the boat accurately represented regardless of how the bottom is viewed.

"You really know where you're putting your pots and there's no question that this system has made us a lot of money. You don't have to go looking at charts any more, you know exactly what you're doing at any time"

Can he actually see the crab? "No way," says Jostein. "You can't see them on the bottom with any kind of instrument, no matter how big the crab are. It's basically impossible. You just set your pots and hope they crawl in."

CHAPTER 12

"I'm too young to retire. This is what I love, this is what I know."

The *Aleutian Number One* came back down to Seattle in early July of 1999 and was hauled out at Marco for fresh bottom paint, minor deck modifications and general maintenance. When the yardworkers opened up the steering compartment in the stern they discovered the main steering arm was hanging by half a bolt. "Ready to break, you're lucky you made that last turn to run her in to the dock."

Ron was still up in Bristol Bay and didn't get back until a week later. I dropped by his house to see how the season had gone. "We did OK. Not great, but good." The run had turned small for the second year and the slowing Japanese economy was beginning to hurt prices.

"Years ago all the Japanese wanted was the Sockeye roe. Then they started buying frozen fish. The way they play the game now, our fish goes to Japan, but we pay the freight over and pay for the cold storage and they take it only as they need it. They don't just buy it and store it for themselves. Nowadays there's farmed salmon from Chile and the Japanese own most of those farms so they're playing one against the other. Our price has gone from two dollars and forty-seven cents in 1988 down to about sixty to seventy cents this year, even though the runs are a lot smaller because of El Nino or some damn thing. There's guys up there that didn't make a dime this year that used to make big money. Bristol Bay permits got up over two hundred thousand a couple of years ago, but they're coming down fast. Guys were putting a quarter of a million into new boats. No way can they make it with that kind of debt."

Ron's house was in Blue Ridge, an upscale hillside residential community about a mile north of Ballard proper. While not the fanciest house in the neighborhood, the place has four bedrooms on the top level and a snazzy two-bedroom apartment downstairs where his son, Kris, had been living until he was kicked out. Both have magnificent kitchens. All with the spectacular view of Puget Sound and the Olympic mountains. Expensively furnished. Gloria had moved out months ago. "She decided she didn't like this house any more. It's going on sale this fall."

Ron fixed me a snack while we talked. Cream cheese and smoked salmon on french bread. Cokes. (A beer would have been nice on this sunny afternoon. Or wine. But neither of us was drinking alcohol at this point. I always tell my wife I'm going back on the sauce on my eightieth birthday. Seven more years!)

He brought me up to date on his deals.

"My option on the waterfront cannery in Anacortes ran out, so I had to let that go. For a million bucks, it was a steal." (Six months later the property did indeed sell for two million, but Ron had planned to develop it, not sell. Oh well.) The *Akutan* was still a headache. Before he had gone north he had come close to a deal with some brokers from Sweden who would put up the dough for converting it to a catcher/processor going after Pacific cod.

"There's a huge shortage of cod in the world and the Bering Sea is one of the few places in the world where there's lots of it left. That boat would have netted a half million a month easy, plus what we could have made processing Sockeye. But when push came to shove these guys wanted fifty-one percent of the deal. Why in hell should I give them a controlling interest when all they had to contribute was money? They didn't know how to catch fish, they couldn't run the damn boat. No way. Come right down to it, I don't think they even had the cash. Then I had some other guys interested, but they wanted it as a tax loss. I had to tell them, Ron Peterson does not go into a deal to lose money. I catch fish and I make money."

So the *Akutan* was on the market. Two million bucks asking price.

"Come on over to Marco with me and let's have a look at the A-1."

On the way over he told me more about Bristol Bay. He had taken his new girlfriend, Linda, and one of her friends up for a week before the season started. Both women had a good time, but Linda's friend was a bit flirty, so she kept attracting unwanted attention that Ron had to sort out. Got to be a bit of a strain—taking two beautiful women to Bristol Bay is maybe one too many. He took them salmon fishing up on the Nushagak River. Caught couple of big kings—one a forty-pounder. Encountered a bear way too close for comfort. Pulled Linda down the trail so hard he sprained her wrist.

We pull into the guard shack at Marco. Ron asks the guy on the gate if he still has his old '64 Caddy. (He did, and promised Ron a ride.) Ron shoots the breeze with the workers as we walk across the yard to the drydock where the A-1 is hauled out. Three years ago she had been in for a complete repaint. "Marco did such a good job that we threw them a crab feed. We did it for the workers—the guys coming on swing shift came in a half hour earlier and the day shift stayed a half hour later—we had to do it all in an hour. And those guys said that all the crab boats they built and worked on they never had anybody throw a feed for them yet. A hundred and eight guys and we went through three hundred pounds of crab, a hundred pounds of salmon and there wasn't nothing left. It was a hit." (Almost a miss because after getting all the food laid out and ready to go, it turned out that somebody forgot to buy charcoal briquets.)

Sitting on keel blocks in Marco's drydock, the A-1 looks absolutely immense. A great, red-bottomed, white-sided steel behemoth, a harvester of the ocean. The bottom paint is soft with a powdery bloom almost an eighth of an inch thick. "They'll sand blast it and then it has to be painted within hours before the steel has a chance to oxidize."

We climb up the ladder to the wings of the drydock and then cross over the gangplank to the boat's deck. Jostein is fashioning a steel pipe safety rail on the bulwark to give the operator of the picking crane a little safer place to stand when it's rough and the boat is rolling hard. He measures and fits then goes below to use the drill press in the engine room. Ron and he exchange perfunctory greetings. ("Did we come here to work or talk.")

The after deck of the A-1 is huge—30-feet wide and 90-feet long. And it's a drydock shambles with gear and tools and hose, line and miscelllaneous crap all over the place. Three or four yard workers going methodically about their various jobs. Everything looks very, very used. The deck is surfaced with two by six Arikara wood planks spaced an inch apart and raised an inch off the surface of the deck for drainage. It's the toughest hardwood they can buy, but a number of the planks have been so damaged and worn down by the pots that they are being replaced.

There are two bait freezers on the port side behind the house, with a bait chopping machine just outside the freezers. The companionway door leads past a washer and dryer. "We always go with a couple of extras aboard because they take a beating." The galley is to starboard with a U-shaped kitchen workspace next to nicely upholstered dinette back in the corner with two rectangular ports that look aft to the working deck. The galley doesn't look 20-years old. Stainless steel electric appliances, lots of well-fitted teak trim and black formica. The table seats eight and has a diagonal slot cut from one corner to the middle of the opposite side so that the men sitting in the back can go out the slot without moving everyone else. Makes sense. Saves a tremendous amount of spilled coffee and bad language. TV, VCR, speakers and tape deck in the outer wall. There are three crew staterooms—two-berthers on either side with a four-berther amidships. Nicely paneled. Tidy. Comfortable. Also with TV's, VCR's, speakers, tape decks.

Down a companionway to the engine room with four—count 'em four-diesel Caterpillers. The big 16-cylinder main. Two smaller 6-cylinder auxiliaries running generators and a big V-8 to run the hydraulics. There's been some talk that the cylinder block of the main engine—which has been completely overhauled twice—may be experiencing metal fatigue after some 70,000 hours of operation. "Cat doesn't make this engine anymore, but they do make the blocks, so we could replace that." I look around this space crammed with machinery and wonder how in hell they'd ever be able to pull the engine. "Just cut a hole in the bow and pull it out the front. Stick the new block back in, weld her back up and you'd never know it had been done." Having a steel boat can be a real advantage.

The after bulkhead of the engine room is mounted with piping and valves and gauges controlling all the fluids on the vessel—fuel, water, and hydraulics—as well as the electrical systems. Marco builds and installs everything on this single bulkhead outside the boat and puts it in complete as a single unit. This makes the boat much easier to build because it avoids all the normal tangled interferences which are inevitably encountered when the builder installs each of these systems separately after a hull is built and enclosed. Having everything neatly organized right there on one bulkhead also makes the vessel much easier to maintain and troubleshoot. "Where in the hell did they put the shut-off valve for the number three bilge pump on this fucking tub?" On the A-1 they know. They know.

A couple of young A-1 crewmen are wrenching away replacing the water pump on the V-8. "Don't forget about our beach party," Ron tells them. "We'll have it unless the Alaskans move up the brown crab season on us. IF THAT HAPPENS WE GOT TO BE

OUT OF HERE IN TWO DAYS! If not, we're going to have that party and don't plan on doing anything else." "You got it, Ron." Like most people they get a kick out of old Ron.

We go up to the bridge. Here as elsewhere, the fit and finish are very nice. Everything shows a lot of thought and skilled attention. Nothing jury-rigged or temporary. No tangles of wire hanging down. Everything tidy. Traditional wooden wheel and compass amidships. Chart table across the after side of the bridge with a couple of massive electrical panels, CD and tape players and speakers, and two HP desk jet printers, traditional clock and barometer.

The skipper's real "office" is to starboard. He sits on a heavy-duty upholstered seat on a swivel pedestal. The vessel is steered with a toggle—a little black ball on a short angled stem which angles out from the rim of a steel disc about the size of a hockey puck. Moving the ball to the left or right actuates the rudder, and a rudder angle indicator shows how far the helm is turned. Twenty different gauges* are mounted on a black plexiglas panel mounted low and at an angle to the lower left of the helm chair. Autopilot. Four radios. Global Positioning System. Loran. Two radars. Computer (with the mouse on a tidy little teak-trimmed shelf at his left hand.) A television screen hooked up to a camera on the back side of the house shows Jostein what's happening on the after deck. About the only low-tech item is a big 8 inch by 18 inch rear-view truck mirror mounted outside the side windows which allows Jostein to see when a pot breaks the surface.

*I noted gauges for engine speed, fuel consumption, exhaust temperature, manifold temperature, lube oil temperature and pressure, gear oil temperature, coolant temperaure, turbo boost main, turbo boost V-8, gear oil pressure, fuel oil pressure, Hertz, AC volts, AC amps, ampmeter selector, lube oil pressure, and generator switches.I may have missed or misread a few.

Jostein comes up to show me how his chart system works. He turns it on and dials up the local Puget Sound chart. Uses the mouse to draw a litle square around Salmon Bay. Punches a few keys and there it is, the screen is filled with a perfect three-dimensional representation of the bottom contour. Then he shows me a chart up in the Aleutians and punches up an area about two miles square where the boat actually fishes. Fiddles with the mouse to view the bottom from different angles. Magic. He doesn't let me study that very long. I believe he thinks I'm a foreign agent.

Skipper's cabin is down a couple of stairs aft of the bridge. Private digs. Private head. But there's an extra pilot chair on the bridge which is obviously a spacious and comfortable place to hang out. The A-1 is blessed to have Cat engines. They're much quieter than the screaming two-cycle GMC's that power many other boats. (I spent five weeks sleeping above a 12-cyclinder Jimmy on an Alaskan coastwise freighter several years ago and my ears are still ringing.)

Ron and I go down to the galley for a Coke. He's a cell phone addict. I tell him about seeing the boat broker's ad for the *Akutan* in Pacific Fisherman magazine that read "Asking $2 million try $1" Ron calls them immediately. I hoped for their sake that it was a typo. I told him about a rental that had just come up at our condo down on Shilshole Bay. Ron gets right on the phone and makes an appointment to see the place that evening. Makes another call to a fisherman pal who wants him to go partners on a condo up at Whistler Mountain. (Loves to ski.) Tells me a bit about his marriage which dismayed him both emotionally and financially. "She said she was going to take me for everything I had, but when it came right down to it, what it basically amounted to was that she could have half of what I owed." Wise smile.

And by the way, Marco's yard bill was going to run about seventy grand.

Cadet Peterson in his ROTC uniform at Seattle University
shortly before he quit college to enlist.

The 32-foot gillnetter tht Ron parlayed into ...

... the spanking new 127-foot Aleutian No.1.

Ron and Gloria with pal at Harrah's in Lake Tahoe

Ron and friends on the day Gov. Booth Gardner (seated)
signed the law legalizing the Ballard insurance pools.

Ron showed Linda another way to catch fish in Bristol Bay.

CHAPTER 13

"We never ate out at restaurants but at home my mother would have these big dinners. Europeans, Polish people around Ballard my mother knew. One of them was a Polish guy who married a German girl who smuggled food to the prisoners—they came to Ballard after the war, raised a big family. I was about nine and I could sit with the men after dinner, sometimes have a little sip of brandy. They would sing this song, maybe it was Polish, maybe Jewish, but it was beautiful and sad. Then a couple of them would roll up the sleeves of their shirts and show me the tatooed numbers on their arms. I remember asking one of them how he managed to come out of the camps alive. And he said. 'Ronnie, first you have to really believe that you're going to live.'"

We had lunch one day in early fall after the A-1 had gone back north. "You know in some ways this has been the worst year of my life, and in some ways it's been the best."

It had certainly been eventful.

Between bad fishing, bad insurance, bad deals, bad permits,

wild kids and a marriage gone south, Ronnie had plenty to worry about and like a leaky boat in a storm, any number of things could pull him under.

In trying to put together the *Akutan* project, Ron persuaded his old banker friend Floyd Unger to come in as a partner and work with him running the office. Floyd had retired to Hawaii in the early '90s. After years in the hurly-burly of fishery industry finance, Floyd bought a grocery store outside of Hilo and basked peacefully in the warm climate and the simple flip-flop-sandals life of an island storekeeper. But after several years, his wife's medical problems cut this idyll short and regretfully, they sold up and returned to Seattle. Peterson had plenty for him to do.

Ron kept an office on the second story of the Alaska Crab Coalition building in the Fremont district just west of Ballard. The large, one-room office had three desks, two big tables and a couple of couches. The walls were covered with photos of various vessels he has owned over the years. Two amazing aerial photos show an incredible tangle of boats and nets at the "combat zone"— the mouth of the Egegik River in Bristol Bay. Large maps of Alaska—bathymetric and topographic—as well as a bathymetric map of the world. Lots of memorabilia. Seafood packages of various vintages. Coffee pot and a bookcase filled with canned foods. Computers and phones, big piles of papers. Large one-gallon plastic containers of candy on the table near the coffeemaker— jellybeans, red licorice whips and two or three others. (Ron buys everything in going-to-sea quantities.) In memory of Hilo, Floyd kept the office at a steady 80 degrees.

I was over there one day soon after I decided to write this book and Ron and Floyd along with an old friend, Tom Slater, were putting together their proposal on the *Akutan*—a very detailed 24-page rundown on the boat, the budget, the potential. The question of the hour was how much should be allowed for fuel consumption. Tom's experience was in managing processors, Ron's in running boats, Floyd's in financing them. It was an interesting, if arcane, discussion. They agreed on a plausible number and moved on.

This was the project that came to naught in the spring of '99 because Ron wouldn't give the Swedes a controlling interest. Then when Ron got back from Bristol Bay that summer he decided to get out from under the *Akutan*. In September, his broker turned up a buyer who was willing to pay $1,750,000, only to discover, when it came time to close the deal, there was a serious problem with the permits. Besides buying the boat, Ron had purchased permits based on the *Akutan's* catch record which would have allowed the vessel to both catch and process cod. But come to find out, the seller—who shall be nameless—had actually sold the permits separately to another party, and the fishery bureaucrats in Juneau had—either in error or complicity—allowed their transfer to a separate buyer. (Bad things that happen to Seattle fishermen in the back offices of Juneau always look suspiciously unaccidental.) Without the accompanying permits, the *Akutan* was just so much iron, a 177-foot white elephant.

So there the *Akutan* sat. The sale blown to hell. Five grand a month moorage. A quarter of a million dollars in unpaid repair bills. Ron's agenda: Try to refinance the *Aleutian Number One*. Fight the bureaucrats for the damn *Akutan* permits. Fight the insurance company for the claim. Sell his damn house. Stall the creditors. Argue with the banks and ex-wife's lawyers. Keep his own lawyers humping. And oh, by the way, the fall Opilio season had been a bust.

That's the bad stuff.

On the good side, Linda, the lady friend he'd taken to Bristol Bay, moved in with Ron and they found a place to lease in our condo on Shilshole Bay—just across and down the hall from our own. Ronnie was delighted with both Linda and his apartment. His view of Puget Sound was more to the north than from his Blue Ridge front room, but it was comfortable, snug and private. And he could still see every vessel that came in or out of the locks, and if it was a fishboat he usually knew who owned it, who built it and how it had been doing.

Linda was something: a shapely full size woman with a rollicking full size personality. They met through friends and the attraction was immediate and intense. She was from Bellevue, Seattle's cross-the-lake suburb. "Raised rich," says Ronnie. Their relationship was interesting. Fortunately, both are Catholic and Ron said her guitar-mass parish in Bellevue was a lot more fun than the sternly conventional St. Alphonsus he was used to in Ballard. When Ron told his mother that Linda was a vegetarian she said, "Your new girlfriend might be okay, but you'd better teach her to eat meat."

Some of Linda's friends took them sailing. Ron thought it was a lot of fun, but those rich young software guys weren't all that interesting. "Take away their laptops and they don't have much in the way of social skills."

Linda's favorite indoor sport is sewing. She designed and made clothes for herself and friends and on a number of occasions astonished Ron by whipping up a dress to go out in that same evening. The second bedroom in their apartment was turned into a serious, full-scale sewing room.

My wife and I are early/early people and Linda and Ron were late-show/later-riser types so we saw surprisingly little of each other even though they lived just down the hall. But Ron and I got together for lunch every now and then and I would get updates on his struggles.

It turned out that the *Akutan* permit situation was as tangled as Balkan politics. Besides the seller's peculation, there was definite evidence of *bungled* hanky-panky on the part of the Juneau authorities. One set of signed papers gave the permits in question to a third party while another set assigned them to Ron. There were a lot of red faces all around and people kept telling Ron to be patient, not to make a big stink, not to sue, everything would be OK.

Ron was sure he would prevail in the end if he didn't bleed to death in the meantime. Threat of legal recourse hung heavily in the air. "It's like when I used to lend guys money. After a while I'd tell them, 'Hey look, I want my damn money'.' And they'd say sure I'll pay you. Then after a couple of days, I'd ask them again. 'Hey look, I really want it, where's my fucking money? ' And they'd stall me again. Finally I'd have to tell them, 'Look, either you pay me my damn money or I'll break your fucking nose.'" And they wouldn't pay me, so the next time I saw them I'd let them have it, wham, right square in the mouth. And they'd stand there with a surprised look on their face with the blood pouring out and tell me, 'I didn't know you were serious.'"

Aggravation.

His house sale was equally frustrating. The listing broker, of course, set the price sky high and despite Seattle's hot housing market—this was the height of the dot-com bubble—the house was not even being shown. And when the former Mrs. Peterson found out it was up for sale, her lawyer swooped in to demand satisfaction.

As if that weren't enough, Ron had purchased brown crab permits two years previously and the payment—$166,000—was due in a couple of months. Through it all, Peterson remained in a state of high energy and high spirits and relentless optimisim if occasional black moods. "Some mornings you get up and you can't get going. I call Floyd up, say 'Floyd, what's my motivation today?'"

He and Linda worked out at the Ballard Health Club regularly. "I weighed over two-seventy before I quit drinking." That happened after his accident in Petersburg in 1980. He was coming back to the A-1 after celebrating the winning two Super Bowl pools when he slipped and fell on the ice, breaking his leg. He lay there passed out for three hours. He woke up and tried to walk the rest of the way to the boat. His body temperature was down to 91degees by the time they got him to the hospital. Bad spiral break. Good time to quit. Four months before he could go fishing again. "Then the first thing I did was wreck my back picking up a net." Working out on Nautilus machines he finally got his weight down to 212. He now weighs about 240, but can still max the whole routine and go around twice. "You don't have to be big to be strong." When the lease on his big black Cadillac sedan ran out in January he issued himself a new one. Just as big, just as black, but brand new. What the hell. Go out in style.

Ron and I had been talking for months about going crabbing for Dungeness and one nice Sunday in February we finally did it, taking along Linda and my wife. He borrowed three professional double-ring flat traps from a friend plus a big rectangular wire trap with a curved top and bottom. We met at 11 and dragged the stuff down to my old Bill Garden wood cruiser and went out in front of Blue Ridge to set the traps. He did everything. I just ran the boat from the bridge. He baited one of the rings with some freezer-burn salmon from his locker and the others with fresh chicken parts. After setting the traps, we went back to the head of the string and turned off the motor and had lunch. Pulled the traps and did pretty good. Crabs loved the salmon, less so the chicken. Did another set with not as good results. Six keepers all told. Linda told us her story: When she was 18 she ran away to New Zealand to marry a pen pal. That lasted three years. She said the country was pretty boring for an American girl from Bellevue. (No malls, not enough people, too many sheep.) "If you go there, tell them you're a Canadian, they don't like Americans." Linda then married a filmmaker, had a couple of boys, now 12 and 16, who spend the school year with their father in Southern California. Linda misses her kids a great deal. Ron and Linda's boys had a rather uneasy relationship as might be expected. "I told them I wasn't their Dad and never would be their Dad, but I'd sure be their friend if they'd play square with me." After a few troubled outings, things smoothed out quite a bit. Big kids, nice kids, but raised as soft as Ron's son Kris had been raised tough. Teenagers are teenagers it turns out.

Ron was full of stories about gillnetting along this shore. "Used to do real good on Kings. Had a tapered gill net, set the shallow end right on shore. Had ninety Kings one night. Used to do good on Silvers too when they were running. Pretty good life. A lot of fun." No fishing like that nowadays of course. Ron, like all local fishermen, blames Judge Boldt and his decision to give the first half of any Puget Sound harvest to the Indians. I don't argue. But.

As we come up to pick a trap, I maneuver the boat so that

Ron in the cockpit can catch the float with the boat hook on the end of the eight foot pike pole. Linda gets in the way. "Look out for this pike pole, Linda. Never turn your back on somebody working with a pole or you could get whacked. See this pole, George? One time I was gillnetting with a friend of mine and I was kind of in a streak of making eyes at his girlfriend. And he got mad at me one day and when I wasn't looking he broke a pole like this right over my head." The pole is one and a half inch diameter oak. Must have been a considerable headache.

CHAPTER 14

"Ronnie loves to ride the roller coaster"
—Linda Cline

Along about this time, Peterson began to get all wrapped up in his plans for organizing another cooperative fleet of Bristol Bay fishermen. Despite the fact that he was—as he later confessed—financially underwater to the tune of approximately four million dollars, despite the fact that lawyers, bankers and creditors were hounding him, Ron's thirst for opportunity was still strong and unslaked.

The previous season in Bristol Bay he had made an extremely fortuitous move. For several years he had been storing his gillnetter, the *Brianne Lynn*, at a Naknek boatyard jovially named the Naknek Yacht Club. During the previous winter, the partners in the yard, Ralph Young and Chuck Allen, got into a sulphurous dispute which ended with both of them rolling around on the ground trying to kill each other. (Chuck, in his late seventies, was using a pipe wrench. Ralph, a decade younger, had a hammer.) Both liked Ron. So Chuck ended up selling him a half interest in the storage yard with the strict, specific, iron-clad, no-way-Jose proviso that Ron would NEVER sell his share to Ralph. It was a no-money-down deal. Ron just had to make payments which basically amounted to not a whole lot more than what he'd been paying for boat storage. Ralph and his wife had built a spacious new steel building on the property which contained—besides their own quarters—inside storage space for the *Brianne Lynn* and a roomy three-level apartment—three bedrooms, kitchen, office, laundry and meeting room—which they leased to Ron on generous terms, giving him first right of refusal to buy, again with the proviso that he would never resell it to Chuck. Sweet.

But wait there's more!

Next door to the yard, a young businessman, John Lowrance, had built a new frozen fish processing facility. John's waste line for piping fish guts and gurry down to the river ran across a boat yard that Trident Fisheries was trying to buy. If Trident got the land, John's waste line would be history. "Suddenly I had a new best friend," said Ronnie. "I told John there was no reason why he couldn't put his line across our property and was he interested in making a deal to process the fish from the co-op that I was trying to put together?" Naturally he was.

So Ron was highly energized all spring, calling up old Bristol Bay fishing friends from San Diego to Sand Point, Alaska, trying to get them signed up to join his co-op. He figured he needed about 20 boats. By joining the co-op, they would agree to pool their catches and sell them to Lowrance's Leader Creek Seafoods which had a contract to supply frozen salmon filets to the Costco chain in the lower U.S. Ron called his co-op Wild Alaska Seafoods which could cover salmon, crab or cod. (As a reformed advertising man, I thought that name was terrific and was surprised that he was able to get the name registered and trademarked.)

So with a new girlfriend and a fresh new project to bite down on, Ron was as happy as a hound dog with a 10-inch soupbone. A number of his creditors were saying they'd be willing to settle his bills for cents on the dollar, but Ron refused to declare bankruptcy and promised them payment in full. "It's hard to have to stall guys who are friends, especially when you know that they need the money too. I hate to have to put them off, but I tell 'em to hang on, they're going to get every cent plus interest. I know I'm going to get that insurance money, and I am pretty damn sure that the *Akutan* permits are either going to get straightened out or I'm going to have a hell of a big-bucks lawsuit against the bank. The house is for sale and the A-1 is a moneymaker. I'm a good gamble."

He and Floyd went back to Washington D.C. in January to arrange a rollover on his *Aleutian Number One* loan with the National Marine Fisheries, and another Seattle bank had given him a short term working capital loan based on the brown crab income. "A couple of months ago, I couldn't figure out how I could possibly last until the first of the year. Well, here it is March and I'm still here."

With all these balls in the air, he was in his glory, but his partner Floyd was beginning to look a little peaked.

Around the first of April, I was in Bad Albert's where I had gone to meet a pal for lunch. Ron and Linda came in and joined Ed Broomfield at a back table. When it became obvious that my friend was a no-show, I accepted their invitation to join them.

All three were in rare form.

Ed Broomfield is a short, husky man of about my age. A master welder, Ed usually sports a couple of days growth of beard on his round, craggy face. He has short, stubby fingers and a wickedly merry sense of humor. (My petite and pretty wife and I were in there one day for lunch when Ed marched straight up to her and very seriously said, "Have you told him about us?')

Ed had been a U.S. Marine Corps sharpshooter in Korea and still carries several pieces of shrapnel in his leg, courtesy of the Red Chinese Army. For many years he taught firearm courses for various local police forces. He is incorrigibly sexist, loves guns, hates liberals, Democrats, Bill Clinton, Al Gore and all bureaucrats. He senses my limp-wristed-liberalism and teases me unceasingly. Samples: "I was listening to KOMO radio yesterday—and you know how liberal they are [they're decidedly not]—and they said that Clinton was going to take away every

gun and put the United States armed forces under UN command."
"Women should not be in the infantry and they should never be
cops." "I have no sympathy for so-called single mothers
whatsoever." Despite his professional Neanderthalism, Ed is a
man of considerable attainments. After Korea he earned a UW
metallurgy degree A widower, he has four kids, two of whom are
partners in the business and a daughter-in-law who bemusedly
sits with him in their tiny office up front. The Broomfield shop
next door is about 20 feet wide by maybe 100 feet long and is
crammed from front to back, floor to ceiling with a mad
conglomeration of tools and pipe. Their specialty is marine
exhaust systems for boats and ships and the work he and his
sons turn out displays truly beautiful, almost elegant
craftsmanship. (Ed and David Smith, the great and equally craggy
metal sculptor, would have appreciated each other.) Ed had the
second biggest English mastiff I ever saw in my life. After lunch
he saved all the scraps at our table for the dog including a big
mound of mashed potatoes and gravy.

Ron and Ed go back a long way and the older man has a
warm-hearted regard for Ron and takes a deep paternal interest
in his struggles. Ron tells Ed that he took Linda to the shooting
range the other day and she did real good with his forty-five. Ed
kids Linda by telling Ron that it was a mistake to let her carry a
pistol. "She shouldn't be allowed to have anything smaller than
a thirty-ought-six rifle so you could tell that she was packing."
Bold, attractive, and outgoing, Linda wants a gun—and the ability
to use it—for the bears she might encounter in Bristol Bay in
June. It's a not unreasonable precaution since Ron won't be
around to protect her when he's out fishing—either from bears or
from two-legged predators.

Ron was full of stories. Many I had heard before, but one or
two were new.

One was about the spotter pilot in Bristol Bay he and a couple
of friends were drinking with one night. Frisky, they all decided
to go up to King Salmon in the pilot's jeep. There were four of
them with Ron and another friend standing up in back holding

onto the roll bar. After whooping it up, they were heading back to Naknek all pretty well loaded. Suddenly the pilot whipped the jeep up a steep sand bank, pitching Ron and his pal off the back. Just for the hell of it, which made them pretty sore. So they climbed back on and started off again. After a mile or so, the pilot did it again, throwing them off again. This time Ron's friend—a guy even bigger than he—was raring to fight. But Ron calmed him down. They were still eight miles from Naknek and the mosquitoes would eat them alive. "The guy was acting real weird besides driving real strange and I asked him what in the hell made him so crazy. He said, 'Hey look boys, I'm sorry, but I had a real bad day.' It turned out that he had been hired to fly a dead body back to Anchorage—some Filippino that had half his head blown off in a gunfight. The plane was almost to Anchorage when the pilot heard a noise. He looked back to see the corpse throwing off the tarp and sitting up straight in his litter and wanting to fight. He was dead by the time the plane landed all right, but the experience and the booze had made the pilot act a little nuts."

Ed and Ron swapped the latest gossip about Chuck Bundrant, the Trident Fisheries tycoon. He had recently snapped up the cream of the Bering Sea catcher/processor fleet which had belonged to Tyson Foods. Now Bundrant had worked another major deal (Federal Law 1221) with Alaska Senator Ted Stevens and then Washington Senator Slade Gorton. This law divvied up the processing and catching of Alaskan pollock in a way that made everybody happy except for the poor independent fishermen. Everybody hopes that Bundrant may finally have bitten off more than he can chew, but that's probably wishful thinking. The way the deal came down, Trident (and a few other majors) were granted both processing quota as well as catching quota. What that meant was that the big boys didn't have to buy anybody else's fish until their own boats and own shore plants had exhausted their own quotas. Short story: "Sorry Ole, we really don't need your fish, but tell you what, we'll take them off your hands for say, oh, two cents a pound. OK?"

Bundrant was a considerable character in his own right and

in the early '90's Ron had partnered with him by managing Bundrant's crabber, the *Dominator*. The partnership dissolved in a dispute which was settled in Ron's favor by an outside arbitrator. This didn't set well with Bundrant. "To this day Chuck's still sore at me, but I still like him," said Ron, "And I really admire his guts. One time he owed a bunch of money to a shipyard back east that was giving him a lot of heat and instead of paying the bill he went to the bank and borrowed enough to buy out the yard." Last year at the annual Seafood Festival at Fishermens' Terminal, Bundrant had himself flown into the party suspended by a rope sling 100 feet under one of his Trident helicopters.

Ron Peterson is obviously not the only character in Ballard.

CHAPTER 15

"George, you really ought to come up to Bristol Bay this summer."

$\mathbf{H}$e didn't have to ask me twice.

Ron, Linda and Floyd were going up to Naknek the first of June. I was to follow a week later. The plan was to spend three or four days watching Ron trying to wire together his co-op and then a couple of days out on the bay aboard the *Brianne Lynn*.

Several years ago when I bummed a ride up to the Aleutians on the old coastal freighter, *Capelin*, we spent time in Bristol Bay loading frozen salmon from the floating processors. So I was able to get a good look at the goings-on from that perspective, but now I was going to see Bristol Bay up close—much closer—from the fisherman's point of view.

I'm not much of a tourist, but I do enjoy traveling somewhere for a purpose. For me, it started getting interesting right at the Alaska Airlines check-in counter at the Seattle-Tacoma International Airport. Alaska's passengers—and their pilots and crews—are an exceedingly various lot. Walk along their Seattle concourse and you'll see normal looking people going to everyday

destinations like Vegas or LA or Spokane. But right at the gate
next door, the folks are headed for fastnesses like Nome, Kodiak,
Cold Bay or Dutch Harbor and strenuous existences which only
a small percentage of today's Americans could envision let alone
endure. Pilots the same way. I know a lady Alaskan Airlines pilot
who keeps a stunt biplane for fun. She calls DC 10's "Gucci
airplanes" and prefers flying the Alaska runs in a 737. She says
she doesn't get really interested until bringing her plane into
Juneau in bad weather. I know another Alaskan pilot—a
comparative wuss—who likes flying up north, but draws the line
at Dutch Harbor. That wee airport is sporty even in good weather.
In bad weather the jets take one look and go right back to
Anchorage.

My own ticket read King Salmon International Airport, change
planes in Anchorage, leave Seattle at noon.

As I chugged my baggage down the serpentine waiting line
to the baggage counter, I got behind two elderly couples with
mounds of luggage headed for Anchorage to join a Princess Tour.
Panic and frustration was writ large on their flushed faces. (I'm
73 myself so I'll make fun of old people if I damn well please.)
One of the husbands went off on some fool errand or other and
hadn't returned by the time they were at the head of the line and
the remaining geezer was hard pressed to scoot all the baggage
to the counter and by this time, the two wives were in full dither.
But they made it okay, and needless to say ended up seated
beside and across the aisle from me when we all finally got on
the crowded 737. And ahead of me in their customary disarray
as we got off the plane. They were sweeties, but I was thankful I
wasn't their caretaker on a tour.

As we flew up, I tried to identify fishermen who might be
going on to King Salmon, and I thought I could spot a few—trim
and purposeful men of various ages. Another large and ebullient
contingent on the plane were heading to a meeting in Anchorage
which turned out to be a Leukemia Convention. Caregivers, I
assumed, certainly not patients or relatives.

Flying to Anchorage can be beautiful. I remember coming

up the coast on a clear winter day with sunlit snow down to the intensely blue water's-edge all the way along the coast. But no scenery this day until the thawing mountainsides behind the city loomed suddenly below as we broke through the clouds coming in.

Anchorage Airport is exotic. Full of over-the-pole jumbos from obscure airlines all over the world stopping by for fuel. Old cargo planes lumbering in and out carrying God-knows-what to God-knows-where. Ancient DC-4's and 6's. Commuter jets. F-16's from adjoining Richardson Air Force Base. Like most airport terminals, Anchorage is in a more or less constant state of reconstruction and rather more than normal confusion.

My King Salmon flight left an hour later. Another 737. Also full, but this time it was with commercial fishermen—happy, excited extroverts going to the world's biggest salmon derby. Strong, hearty, healthy-looking blokes of all ages including a sprinkling of natives and Filipinos. The one-hour flight to King Salmon headed west and south across Cook Inlet, the least inspiring body of water in Alaska, muddy and punctuated by oil platforms with their orange plumes of burn-off natural gas. Over the mountains and across the Bristol Bay tundra flats, potholed and still winter brown.

King Salmon "International" was a mob scene—almost everyone was being met and picked up. The tiny terminal is a one-story frame building. Two-man ground crew, one lady ticket agent. Baggage was unloaded into a huge three-sided plywood box on a forklift, then brought over and unloaded into a fenced stockade next to the terminal. Lots of coolers duct-taped shut holding meat on dry ice for fishboat crews. Every last bit of baggage had to be unloaded and deposited in the stockade before the gate was finally unlocked. Then a big friendly hullabaloo as everybody dove in to find their stuff.

Ron and Linda met me in the terminal. Linda in her very dramatic long black coat with the appliqued Haida designs on the scarlet lapels. Ron in an old tan parka with black nylon windpants, high top Adidas. He saw lots of old friends as we waited for my bags. Introduced me to Uncle Squash—Joe Papetti from San Francisco. At eighty-three he's said to be the oldest active skipper in the Bay. Sixty-seven seasons, most always with female crew and many times the highliner. Foxiest grandpa afloat. There's a gift shop next to terminal. Ron knew the ladies who run it. Introduced me to one and all. "This is my friend, George. He's writing a book about me." I tried not to cringe. (I'm not used to posing as an author, and having read this far, you know why.) But Ron was happy. In his element.

After we got my bags—one for me, one for Ron with some extra duds he'd asked me to bring along plus a couple of high-powered cattle prods for Linda's protection instead of a 30.06—we piled into the old '79 Chevy Suburban that Ron leases for the season. King Salmon is tiny. A few restaurants, a couple of motels. Alaska Fisheries Building. The airport. Some stores. That's about it. Odds and sods of little businesses strung sparsely along the two lane highway leading to Naknek 15 miles away. Blink twice and you're out of town, but there are quite a few buildings out in the bush including the old King Salmon Air Force Base and several fair-sized resort hotels for sports fishermen. The spindly little spruce trees thin out after a few miles and if you squint a little, the area looks like so much North Dakota. Mostly flat. A few dips now and then.

Ron loves it. To him this is gorgeous country. "This new paved road is great. It was frost-heaved gravel until a couple of years ago. Rougher than hell." I guess it's time to mention that Ron is an unusual, that is to say terrible, driver. His heavy foot bounces on and off the accelerator constantly and he uses both sides of the highway as he talks a mile a minute, looking left and right and waving his arms. (Floyd told me later that Ron had never had a new car that did not need a new transmission before the drive train warranty had expired.) I had jumped in the front seat at the airport, but soon wished I was sitting in the far back seat. I don't normally use a seatbelt, but lashed myself in very carefully from then on. He gets kidded a lot about his driving and more than one friend won't ride with him. Ron mentioned that he had put a "scratch" on his new Cadillac the week before he left. Later I heard him on the phone with the insurance adjuster in Seattle. He had a very plausible story, and naturally, he had not been drinking. But I don't think any insurance agent who ever rode with him would give him coverage. It's amazing to me that he avoids serious collisions. Two nights after I arrived, he and Linda were coming back from a late dinner when a Naknek cop pulled them over and told Ron had been over the center line seven times in three miles. "Give me a breathalizer, officer, I haven't had a drink of any kind in over eight years." Got off without a ticket.

Halfway to Naknek, we pulled off the highway and went down a gravel road toward the river. "I want to show you the land I bought last year." It's four wide-open acres right on the river. Next door there's a weatherbeaten little brown bungalow owned by the former mayor of Naknek. Ron's piece has a gentle slope down to the river with about a twenty foot bank. There's a sparse grove of birches and alders at the edge of the bank, thinned out to improve the neighbor's view up the river. Oddly enough in all this spacious desolation, property is hard to come by. Most of it is zoned out or belongs to natives. Ron plans to build a year-round log cabin. Rent it out in the winter to a schoolteacher, use it himself in the summer. As a property owner he would be allowed a subsistence gillnet in the river in front of his land. Set it at high tide, go pick the fish when low tide leaves the net high and dry. It would pay the taxes and then some. Linda hurt her ankle in the soft tundra and sat uncomplainingly in the sun as Ron and I explored his spread.

We drove into Naknek, a year-round settlement of some 300 souls that puffs up to around 10,000 for six weeks a year. The maps call it a town, but actually it's not even a wide spot in the road. Just a string of modest roadside stores and businesses spaced out along about two miles of highway on the north side of the Naknek River. The town gas station is a single pump in front of a small shack. A scattering of houses and other structures on sideroads out in the bush. Boats of all descriptions and vintages scattered through the area, on both sides of the road, alongside houses, in vacant lots, wherever. Some are active, some for sale, some abandoned old wooden double-enders. Also lots of dead and dying pickup trucks and vans plus the classic weatherbeaten detritus that decorates almost every Alaskan village and town. But along the road or out in the weeds, there's everything the fishermen might need, including the Red Dog Saloon and Inn. Most buildings have a bleached-out, wind-lashed look. Eight or nine months of gales and blizzards take their toll.

The city dock, oil dock, and canneries are along the riverfront with old bunkhouses next to the canneries. With the season due to open in four days, Naknek was humming. I even spotted a couple of joggers on the road and a rudimentary espresso stand— what's Alaska coming to?

We stopped at one of the two groceries in town. Ron ran into three young fishermen trying to buy rubber boots. "You're at the wrong store. Come on, I'll give you a ride down to the Naknek Trading Company, they've got 'em." As we drove, Ron pitched them on joining his Wild Alaska Seafoods co-op and they didn't know what to make of this overwhelmingly enthusiastic character. He obviously knew his stuff, but came on stronger than they could deal with. Ron helped them find their boots at the Trading Company which is a grocery store with hardware, sporting goods, outdoor clothing and appliances on the side. "Come on, I'll give you a ride to your boat." "No, no, that's OK." They set off down the road with their new boots wondering who in hell that big dude was and whether or not they've passed up a good deal.

Ron wanted to see what was going on at Trident, drove up the road another mile or so and pulled into their yard where more than 100 boats are stored next to the cannery. We went into the company store to buy a couple of new knives and swap a little gossip with the store manager who Ronnie knew from Ballard. Trident's President—and Ron's former partner—Chuck Bundrant now has the biggest fishing combine in the state with fishboats, processors and canneries—and big chunks of quota for all three. At Bristol Bay it works like this: Trident stores the boats for the independent fishermen, sells them insurance, fuel, and supplies. Convenient. But by the time they go in the water, most of them are so far in hock that they have to take the company price on their fish and are afraid to sell elsewhere. The real kicker is when Trident says, as they did last year, "Boys, we've got more fish than we can handle, so we're going to have to put you on limit. And oh yes, just 40 cents a pound." Strong men weep and curse, but that's the deal. Hard cards.

Leaving Trident, we drove back to the Naknek Yacht Club, home of Wild Alaska Seafoods, Ron Peterson, President.

Ron introduced me to Chuck Allen. During the winter, Chuck has built himself a tidy little 12 by 16-foot building overlooking his personal launching ramp at the edge of the narrow little notch in the riverbank they call Leader Creek. One room, with a thick shag carpet, couch and easy chair. Comfy. Chuck doesn't look too good. He's portly, red-faced, a little puffy. He's had a heart problem and is still recovering from major surgery. But he's jovial and cheerful with a wickedly crafty gleam in his eyes and a handshake like iron. He had been a big gambler in his day and tells stories about playing rat-pack poker in Vegas with Sinatra and the boys. Chuck's launching ramp takes care of off-site boats from up and down the road. His ex-partner, Ralph Young, has a separate ramp fifty feet down the creek and he only handles the boats stored on the yard premises. Ralph and Chuck still aren't speaking, but both get along great with big Ronnie.

Ralph and Chuck have identical launching rigs—low-slung eight-wheeled trailers with two long steel arms. The trailers are towed around by big, middle-swiveled diesel loaders with six-foot tires. To launch a boat—all 32-footers remember—the trailer is backed under the boat which rests on square steel support tubes with plywood pads at the hull and in the dirt. Hydraulic support pads powered by a ten-horse lawnmower engine on the front of the trailer raise the boat off its blocking. Then the boat is trundled down to the ramp and backed into the water until it floats. The front tires of the loader go in the water up to the hubs. It's all pretty much like a sport fishermen's launching ramp, only big boats, big gear. Slick. The only problem is the tide. Leader Creek is shallow as well as narrow and at least a 16 foot tide is needed for the boats to float free. The extreme tidal range up here goes from minus 3 feet to plus 28 feet with two highs and two lows every 25 hours, each tide occuring approximately 40 minutes later every day. Getting all the boats launched that want to go in while there's still enough water can be a real hassle. When the tide is going out it's like somebody pulled the plug in a bathtub. The loader drivers are cowboys and they hump their rigs around the yard with speed and dispatch. Chuck's man, who sports a goatee and drooping fu manchu mustache, boasted to me that he once launched 25 boats in a single tide. Who am I to doubt it?

Ralph's new building is a three-story structure sheathed in blue corrugated steel. Ralph and his wife live in an apartment on the top floor on the end toward the river. Below him are two floors of rented-out bedrooms for boat crews and a big communal kitchen, bath and washroom. (Thus, the Naknek "Yacht Club") Ron's section is toward the road. Kitchen and laundry/bathroom on the ground floor along with the big dry-storage room for the *Brianne Lynn*. Ron's office, bedroom and bath are on the second level, with two bedrooms and a large TV room on the third floor. We enter via a stairway to the office where we take off our shoes to keep from tracking boatyard sand all over the floors.

There's nothing fancy about the place, but plain and dry and clean count for a great deal in Naknek. Also warm. Windows are small and triple glazed and the window sills are a good ten inches wide which give evidence of the thickness of the heavily-insulated walls.

I threw my dufflebag in one of the upstairs bedrooms, picking a bunk next to the window which looks over the ten boats stored between the building and the road. Ron wanted to go up and see how John Lowrance was getting along at his processing plant next door.

CHAPTER 16

"The main thing is having a home for your fish."

Leader Creek Fisheries didn't look like much. It was a sprawling one-story steel building just off the highway. Out under a shed roof in front were a couple of large, open concrete tanks set in the ground like swimming pools to hold the salmon in refrigerated salt water for processing. The salmon would be offloaded from John's tenders at his dock anchored a couple of hundred feet out in the river. There a fish pump on the dock would suck the salmon out of the tender's tanks and propel them through a 12-inch pipe suspended from piling into tanks mounted on a truck.on the shore. Then they would be driven up to the plant and dumped into the holding tanks.

Lowrance turned out to be a young, mild-mannered guy in coveralls. He and his young Swiss engineer showed us around. They were in the last stages of converting the operation over to salmon after processing 300 tons of Togiak herring the previous month. Looking at the empty plant, it was hard to believe that a hundred people would be cleaning, portioning and freezing salmon here in less than a week. The gear in the backrooms was impressive. Big diesel generators, big freezer compressors, big hydraulics and electrical panels. It turns out that it takes a lot of heavy and expensive machinery to produce that demure little one-pound frozen filet in your grocery cold case. Plus some remarkably ingenious processing equipment. And impressively deft and skillful knifewielding workers on the line. John's deal was with Orca Seafoods which had the contract with Costco for frozen Sockeye filets. They'd take everything Leader Creek Fisheries could process. And Lowrance would take all the salmon that Ron's Wild Alaska Seafoods fleet could catch. That was the deal.

Ron's challenge was to catch the fishermen.

After fishing the bay for 35 years, he was convinced that peak runs came every five years. Although the five-year cycle certainly *had* been the pattern, the state's biologists were not so sanguine about the year 2000. They were predicting a catch of just 22 million fish—about half as many as 1995. (That had been Ron's all-time best year—230,000 pounds of Sockeye at $1.50 a pound.)

But nowadays there was considerably less processing capacity on the Bay. And last year, 1999, even with a rather light catch of 25 million fish, Trident had put its fishermen on quota half way through the season. Ron had tried to organize a co-op last year with little success, but after Trident announced quota, Ron suddenly had a lot of friends. "They came knocking on my hull when we were at anchor at night, 'Ronnie, where you been, I've been trying to call you for weeks.'"

Here's how the new Wild Alaska Seafoods co-op was going to work.:

"A" boats that signed up now would be guaranteed a home for all the fish they could catch, the price based on the highest two prices in the Bay, plus a five cents per pound bonus at the end of the season. "A" boats would also each get a 2.48% equity in Wild Alaska Seafoods. So far Ron had seven boats signed up and was aiming for 15.

"B" boats wouldn't get a share in the company, but if they

sold their first 20,000 pounds of salmon to Leader Creek, Ron would guarantee a home for all the fish they caught above that. He had a lot of guys interested, but at that point, no firm commitments.

So about the time I hit the scene, Ron was striving with might and main to sign up fishermen, hawking his deal up and down the road to everybody he met. Lowrance, besides working frantically to get ready, had his fingers crossed that Ron would be able to find enough boats to supply enough fish to make all his effort and investment pay off. Big gamble all the way around.

Fortunately, Peterson loves challenge. Hey, that's why he fishes. That's why he can't help thinking up new ways to stick his neck out. Up in Bristol Bay, at least he had it down to one set of balls in the air: 1) trying to sign up more boats, 2) getting the *Brianne Lynn* ready to go 3) working out final arrangements with John, 4) keeping Chuck and Ralph happy, 5) teaching Floyd the ropes on the office side, 6) keeping Linda amused and out of trouble, 7) handling his crewmen, Todd Hutchinson and son, Kris (who was highly resentful of Linda). What fun! But Ron was happier than I had seen him in months. To him, Bristol Bay is a summer vacation.

Three of Ron's A-fleet boats sat just outside the entrance to the office. Their owners and crew slept on their boats as they readied their nets and worked on their gear, but as old friends, they had the use of the kitchen, head and laundry.

Ron Brill was half-owner of the *Floodtide* with Peterson. From Lake Sammamish outside Seattle, he also owned two crab boats. A big easygoing guy, about Ron's age, he still took a nip or two. As did his pal, Bob Smith, a short, blond-haired fellow, also from Seattle. Last year they had been out on the town, enjoying Naknek nightlife, when driving back to their boat at high speed, they missed a turn and flew 80 feet off the road slamming into the muskeg so hard that Brill's head poked a large bump in the roof and and equally large dent in his head. Although they had been fortunate to survive, he and Bob regarded the accident as a great joke. "That damn truck was stuck in the muskeg up to the hubs."

(Linda called them the crash-test dummies.) The third member of *Floodtide's* crew was a quiet young Aleut from Lake Illiama, the magnificent headwater lake of the Nushagak River. He was presently living with his girlfriend in Park City, Utah, working as a carpenter. His ancestors had fished Bristol Bay for centuries and like the salmon, he returned every summer. Everybody in Bristol Bay has a story.

Next to the *Floodtide* was the *Sluice Box*, owned by Konrad Schaad. He and his eleven year old son lived in Homer, Alaska and fished their boat by themselves. Born in Switzerland, Konrad told me that he learned to fish with his father, gillnetting salmon at the Swiss Rhinefall. Konrad and his son patiently worked on nets and gear carefully spread out on a blue plastic tarp aft of their boat. Sand and frequent rainsqualls made their work more difficult.

Outside the *Sluicebox* was *Cadenza*, Sam Daniel owner, also with a son along, but only eight years old and making his first trip to Bristol Bay. Sam had been the principal of the Junior High School in Girdwood, Alaska but he and his wife now ran a property management business in the town. Soft-spoken and highly-organized, Sam was Ron's complete opposite. But the two went back a long way as I was later to discover.

After we got back to the apartment, I chatted with Floyd Unger. His office was behind a counter just inside the entrance. Ron and Linda's room and bath were off the office. Being connected to Seattle by computer, Floyd was still wrestling with Ballard loose ends. He and Ron were an odd combination. Floyd the square bear—a clean-living, clean-talking conservative man who listens to Christian radio. (Like Ron, however, he also packed a small pistol while in Bristol Bay.) He was exceedingly loyal. "We've been pushing the string these past few months, but it makes me mad to see the way some people treat Ron and what they say about him."

Linda had planned to do a lot of sewing while Ron was out fishing. But the airline had lost a large carton containing her yard goods and sewing machine. BIG problem, many phone calls, much concern. It finally turned up in Miami, Florida and by the time it got to King Salmon two days later the well-traveled box was about to fall apart but the contents were miraculously undamaged. The other major problem at Wild Alaska Seafoods was cell phones. There was a guy in Naknek who provided the phones, but they proved to be unreliable and mismatched. Linda had ordered new ones from Anchorage, but they hadn't arrived. Ron was getting very uptight—he kept telling her he HAD to have cell phones to coordinate the fleet, the tenders and the plant. Floyd and Linda weren't worried, which made Ron even more uptight.

Along about eight that evening, Ron announced that he was going to cook dinner. The kitchen is large—two reefers and a freezer, table for eight. Overflowing with supplies, tons of canned goods and candy, Big quantities of everything to last the season, shipped up from Seattle in a couple of oversize plywood boxes. Ron, Floyd and Linda had made a huge raid at Costco for this stuff, and apparently that had been quite a scene in itself, but Ron is used to provisioning boats for long trips and knows what to buy and how much. (Tons of snacks, salami by the yard, candy by the gallon.) We sat around the kitchen watching Ron cook the rainbow trout he and Floyd had caught the night before. The trout were two and three pounders. He cut them up into large chunks, then dredged them a shallow glass casserole dish a half inch deep in flour, with lots of salt, and Johnny's Dock seasoning. Then he fried them in about a half inch of olive oil. Much more delicious than I ever would have thought and not a hint of either oil or salt. "Fish need salt!" says Ron. Green beans, salad, rice complete the meal. Ron likes to cook. "A cook can always get a job, right Floyd?"

Kris and Todd had joined us for dinner. Todd is an affable chap, tall, slender, dark haired, in his late thirties. He had fished with Ron off and on for several years. Unmarried, hip, sort of a mature rock and roller, Todd was also a good cook and handyman and had been taking care of Ron's place in Blue Ridge. Up here, he was also pretty much in charge of Kris who was surly and uncommunicative and obviously antagonistic to both Linda and his father. After dinner, there was a very loud argument upstairs between Ron, Kris and Todd. They wanted to go partying but Ron put his foot down. "You go drinking and you're going home! And if either of you goes back, you both go back." Ron is hard on Kris. Kris is hard on Ron. He'd been coming up here since he was eight, fishing with Ron and Grandpa Knute until the old man died in Norway. Last year he had jumped ship on Ron after they had it out in the parking lot over Kris' drinking. So he got on with another boat and ended up quitting because his skipper was drunk all the time. Basically Kris was as difficult as he dared to be. In his defense, it's not easy for a sapling to grow in the shade of a big, old oak tree.

Dishes done and quiet restored, I decided to turn in. Later that night a loud noise woke me that sounded like somebody moving furniture. I stepped out in the hall to see where the racket was coming from and realized that it was just Floyd snoring next door.

CHAPTER 17

"Half the people up here think I'm rich, the other half think I'm broke."

I woke up early, around five, dressed and had myself some cereal, a peanut bar, a glass of milk and a cup of tea. No teapot, so I boiled the water in a saucepan. Tap water up here is about the color of weak boullion and smells a little like it too. Tea tasted kind of interesting. It was a nice morning, so I took a long walk around the old Leader Creek boatyard down by the river. It was quiet at this early hour. I counted over 100 gillnetters on blocks in three long lines. Many of them had crews sleeping aboard, wisps of smoke coming from their stove stacks. The Leader Creek Boathouse is the largest structure—an old empty wooden barn of a place big enough to shelter probably twenty or thirty boats. Sand floor. Four heads, and a couple of scabrous showers to serve the needs of all the fishermen whose boats were hauled out in the yard.

There are two branch outlets of Ballard chandleries on the premises. Lots of containers and small net lockers scattered here and there. A propeller shop. Some trailers. Old pickups and odds and sods of boat gear everywhere. The whole place has a wonderful maritime ad-hoc messiness about it. Down alongside the creek between the two launch ramps, there's a good-sized empty building that had been a store, but Trident now owns it and according to Ron, they keep it empty so nobody else can use it. Trident is trying, of course, to buy the entire property but the deal is in litigation for some reason or other. If they are able to take over, the whole layout would probably become both more organized and more expensive.

By the time I got back, Ron was down in the kitchen having breakfast and making his pitch to an old friend named George Venarossa, an ex-heavyweight boxer from Sitka. Tall and slender for a heavyweight, he never made it big in the ring, but was good enough to be the sparring partner for Jimmy Ellis and Larry Holmes. "All those black cats and me the only white guy." George has a nice, gentle humorous manner. He came to Alaska 16 years ago. Still goes back to Pennsylvania every winter to visit his 76-year-old mother. Venarossa fished for Trident and wasn't sure about signing on with Ron. He said they had promised him there were not going to be any new boats, but the last time he went to the mess hall he ran into three new fishermen. Even though he didn't trust Trident, he couldn't quite bring himself to make the jump. Ron kept pitching. Later he signed up as a B boat which Ron was very happy to see. He likes Venarossa.

A little later we went over to visit the net yard where Ron buys and stores his nets. It's a family operation—Charlie and Leila Adams, and two sons in their forties, Kevin and George. Mrs. Adams showed us around. Besides making, repairing and storing nets they fish a couple of their own boats as well. They employ over a dozen workers and produce approximately 500 nets or "shackles" a year. Each net is 150 feet long and two nets shackled together is now the maximum allowable length in Bristol Bay. They buy and stock nylon web in all the fashionable colors—translucent greens, blues and tans.

"Hanging" net is mind-numbing work. The web comes in six-foot widths but must be tied to a float rope at the top and a lead-cored rope at the bottom to make the net hang straight up and down in the water like a curtain. The net hangers sit side by side at benches As they work along the edges of the mesh, they hook each square over a finish nail pounded in the end of a board at the end of their bench and deftly tie the line on with a special hitch knot. They work in silent concentration, but Mrs. Adams said they often get to squabbling over who's slowing the other down and must be separated.

The Adamses have a nice sense of place and history. One wall of the net shed is covered with memorabilia—oars and gear from the old wooden sailing double enders. Mrs. Adams was born in Pittsburg, California, the fishing community at the mouth of the Sacramento River on San Francisco Bay. Mr. Adams is from New York—he learned his trade from his father who made Hudson River shad nets. Kevin took me out back to their living quarters for coffee and showed me a wonderful video of the old Pacific American Fisheries operation. (After I got back from Korea in 1955, my first job in advertising was with a little Seattle agency that handled the PAF account. I cut my teeth writing ads for their Deming brand pink salmon.) PAF had been a giant in Alaska— the Trident of their era. But they folded after statehood. If the state wouldn't let them keep on doing things their way—using fishtraps for example—they refused to play.

After we got back to the world headquarters of Wild Alaska Seafoods, Ron rounded everybody up to go to lunch. We all piled in the Suburban with Linda in front, Floyd and I in the middle, Todd and Kris in the back and away we went. First we had to stop at the old Peter Pan Seafoods bunkhouse at the far end of the town where Kris wanted to see the skipper he crewed for last summer about a couple of hundred dollars in bonus money he still had coming. No dice. Kris came out from the bunkhouse fuming. The guy who owed him money said come back Monday. Kris was muttering dire threats. Ron pooh-poohed him, but Kris was a powder keg of a teenager. Nearly as tall as his dad, Kris had been raised tough. Besides coming to Bristol Bay since he was eight, he had been in kickboxing class since he was twelve.

"When he was sixteen he fought the Pacific Coast Champion and came pretty close to winning." Ron had told me that he and Kris couldn't fight each other in fun any more—one of them was going to be hurt. "But I still have to teach him how to get out of it when somebody really has you down." Almost all serious fights are won or lost on the ground says Ron.

Ron figured he personally got into about thirty or so fights up here over the years. (I ran into a guy at the yard who offered to tell me wild stories about Ron, but I passed—I wanted them first hand.) Coming by the old Whitney Seafoods bunkhouse reminded him of one of them. He was drinking at the Red Dog late one night when he got into a fight that started when a girl—who was with somebody else—groped his crotch. Ron was trying to pull her hand away, (this part I only partly believe), when her boyfriend saw it and punched Ron. So they had it out. Then it stopped. Then the guy slugged Ron again. Same deal. Then the third time. Had it out once more. "I really had to keep pounding on the guy to make him stop." Ron said he got back to the Whitney bunk house around five. Two hours sleep. "You had to show up for breakfast at seven or you were a wuss no matter what you did the night before. I'm sitting there with my dark glasses over my two black eyes staring at my plate when I notice this guy across from me also looking very beat up and also wearing dark glasses. It's the guy I had the fight with. We both take off our glasses, shake hands and laugh it off. No hard feelings."

We ate at Naknek's best and only restaurant, the D and D. At this time of year, it's a busy place. Like any kind of store or commercial establishment in the area, you enter through a wooden-floored vestibule—a place to stomp the sand, mud or snow off your feet and keep out the cold. There's a community bulletin board on the wall, and Ron stops and carefully studies each and every bulletin board he sees wherever he goes. Two things interested him on this one—a 10-by-12 building for just three grand that would have made a good extra bunkhouse and an outfit down near King Salmon that sold smoked halibut. He wrote down both phone numbers. Floyd was relieved that Ron didn't have the time—or the spare three grand—to pursue the bunkhouse deal.

Ron bounded into the D and D with customary brio and bonhommie, jovially greeting the cook, the waitress and two boothsful of old friends. "I have more fun sober than most people have drunk." he said as we sat down. Our waitress, Crystal, was a jolly, middle-aged lady with tightly marcellled blond hair and a German accent. She wouldn't say which, but Crystal was either the girlfriend, wife or caregiver of Uncle Squash—Joe Papetti—whom I had met at the King Salmon Airport. Much kidding about this. "Are you going to fish with him this year?" "No, he has a new girl to do that." Much laughter over the fact that last year Uncle Squash was too old to climb over the gunwale and had to be lowered into his boat in a fish bag.

Lunch was a lot of fun except that Kris, who was seated next to Ron and across from Linda mouthed silent insults to her throughout the meal. Not wanting to start a riot right then and there, Linda kept her own mouth shut. I caught a glimpse of it myself, but didn't say anything. So we got out of there without incident, but the bad blood between son and girlfriend was palpable.

Ron wanted to show me more of the sights, so we drove out to the Naknek airstrip. There is no hangar. Small planes of a wide variety of makes, vintages, and states of repair were strewn up and down both sides of the strip. I spotted an old wingless and gutted Grumman Widgeon perched forlornly between two scrub willows. The strip is well used even in winter—kids from South Naknek are flown back and forth across the river every day to attend school—and many of the planes had big fat tundra tires.

We drove out to the end of the road to the lookout atop a fifty foot bluff at Pederson Point. (Different spelling, same nationality, no relation.) It's an uninspiring sight. The far shore is low and featureless, about twelve miles across the shallow bay. A few boats are out, but no fishing yet. By Monday, there would be all kinds of activity out there.

Ron drove us over to the Naknek Consolidated School—300

students from first through twelfth grade. It was open so we went in to have a look around. It's a nice modern school, spacious, clean and tidy. Between the oil royalties and various Native revenues and dispensations, there's no shortage of money for education in Alaska. Big gymnasium. Banners on the wall celebrating state high school basketball championships—boys *and* girls—in 1990 and 1991.

One more stop, this time at the Post Office. Linda had been dispatched up here the day before to see if the Post Office Notary Public would please come over to Leader Creek to notarize all the buyer authorization certificates at one time so Ron's fishermen wouldn't have to traipse up to the Post Office one by one. Linda had told Ron the notary had flatly refused. Much banter, so Ron said, "I'll go talk to her myself. Is she good looking?" Linda said, "Well, get her hair done and clean her up a bit and I'd say she's pretty nice for Naknek." While Ron and Floyd went in, Linda and I and the boys waited in the car and she confided that the gal is a bleached blond about fifty and weights at least 300 pounds. Ron came out and said, "Yeah, she'll do it, I invited her to come over for dinner." (She never came, but fortunately Ron Brill knew a lady notary at a nearby cannery who liked Brill enough to come over and do the favor.)

That evening, Ron again gave me a lesson in fish cookery. This time it was nice fresh filets from a six pound Sockeye. He baked them at 375 degrees for 30 minutes in aluminum foil. Lots of olive oil, salt and season salt. I'm sold.

After dinner a young fisherman from Bellingham, Dylan Huff, came in to talk to Ron. He was a computer tech ten months a year but had been coming to Bristol Bay since he was in high school. Ron gave him both barrels. "Other co-ops have been a failure because the managers took big salaries off the top. I don't pay myself anything. Floyd gets equity but no salary. We're in it to make a success." Dylan figured there must be a catch, but he can't figure out where. When I turned in, Ron and Dylan were still going at it.

CHAPTER 18

"No future in it anymore."

—*Joe Papetti*

I had gone to bed around nine, rose at five and was having myself a little breakfast (peanuts and fruit cup) when Floyd came down to use the head. He told me that after working out in the high school gym last evening, Ron and Linda ended up going down to King Salmon to see a local chanteuse put on a show at the Ponderosa Inn. They had run into Captain Sam Liberadi and a bunch of the San Francisco Bay Italians who had invited us to their traditional start-of-season barbecue that afternoon.

When Ron came down for breakfast he was bouncing with enthusiasm. They'd had a great time. The singer, "Kira", turned out to be the good-looking wife of a local sport fishing guide who put on a hell of a show. Played the guitar, sang folk songs, show tunes, rock, the works. Did a great Tina Turner. But the big news was the Italians. "Being invited to their barbecue is huge, a real honor. We had quite a talk last night and my hunch is that they want to join the co-op. Twelve boats!"

Ron goes back quite a ways with the Italians who come to

Bristol Bay. He likes them, they like him. Several years ago, a couple of his Italian friends-ex '49er linemen—invited him down to go fishing for striped bass in the Sacramento River. "Me and the two of them and another friend of theirs went up the river to one of their favorite little side creeks and they hauled out an illegal gillnet. I said, 'My God, you guys, I'm a commercial fisherman and I'd be in deep shit if we got caught. The other guy said, 'You think that's bad, hell, I'm a federal judge.'"

The barbecue wasn't until three. In the meantime, Ron called a meeting with the owners he'd signed up so far and got them assembled down in the kitchen around 10 a.m. to go over the deal again. The painfully well-organized Sam Daniel was exasperated by Ron's arm-waving enthusiasm and gave signs of wanting to take over the meeting. This annoyed Floyd, but didn't faze Ron a bit. After going through everything one more time, Ron dragged everybody up the street to take a tour of the processing operation. John Lowrance showed them all around and they seemed impressed and satisfied. There was to be one more meeting on Sunday afternoon.

Another lunch at the D and D. Ron told Crystal that we were going to the Italian barbecue. Any advice? "Keep your mouth shut and only believe half of what you hear." Another attempt was made to collect Kris's money. More stalling. We went back and messed around at the office. An eager young fellow came knocking at the door looking for a crew position. Ron said, "Sorry, full up," but sat him down and told him how to go about getting on: "Don't worry about the dough, just say, 'Let me show you what I can do.' and then pitch in and make yourself useful. I've been in the yard all by myself busting my pick trying to get my boat ready and had guys walk up and stand there watching and ask me if I knew of anybody who needed any help."

When it was time to head out for the barbecue, Ron grabbed ten pounds of snowcrab out of the freezer to take along. Then on the way we stopped by to buy five pounds of the smoked halibut he'd seen advertised on the D and D bulletin board. The smokery turned out to be a small resort near King Salmon owned by a diminutive German blonde in her fifties and her not-so-small but considerably younger girlfriend. Their smoked halibut was terrific. (Their smoked salmon less so.)

The Italian neighborhood—"Garlic Gulch"—is about halfway between Naknek and King Salmon down a dirt road. There were a few small houses off in the bush and one lane dirt driveways gave evidence of more that couldn't be seen. Four gillnetters already rode at anchor in the river. Liberadi's place is a big, two-story corrugated metal building similar to the Naknek Yacht Club layout. The ground-floor boathouse was large enough to shelter four gillnetters and had bunk and bath accommodations for up to twenty crew. Upstairs at one end was the apartment. Ron, Linda, Floyd and I tromped up the stairs and were warmly greeted by Liberadi, a man in his early sixties who, like Ron, had been coming here all his life. Down south he owns a big tuna boat. One year he brought it to the Bay and tried to buy fish. The canneries black-balled anybody who sold to him. That was the end of that.

Having arrived promptly at three, we naturally are first to arrive. Sam and his partner Angelo have a mess-hall-size pot of pasta sauce cooking on the stove. Ron jumps right in and has himself a roaring good time fixing smoked halibut and cream cheese on half slices of french bread. He shows the boys how to crack snow crab—white side down, crack it near the joint, the meat pulls out in one nice long piece. Linda—equally jolly and gregarious—pitches in to help out.

Sam shows Floyd and me around the place proudly. He and his partner had built it themselves over a period of three years. Big kitchen and living room with an adjoining deck overlooking the river, three good-sized bedrooms. One for Sam, one for his partner, one for guests—they were expecting Joe Montana next week.

Sam is very interested that I was writing a book about Ron. He talks my arm off about the book he wants to write. His *grandfather* fished Bristol Bay as well as his father and he himself had been coming here since the fifties. In the old days they started the season working on the square riggers in San Francisco Bay getting them ready, then sailing all the way up, fishing, loading the ship and sailing all the way back. Nine back-breaking months, start-to-finish.

Sam has great stories. Tells me about being on the gillnetter's councils. In the old days it was the Wops versus the Squareheads and the canneries did nothing to stop the squabbles and animosities between the Italians and the Scandinavians. "When I got to be the president of the council, I went out and bought myself a copy of Roberts' Rules of Order and studied it. But when I stood up in front of everybody that first time, I told them that I may not know much about running a meeting, but by God I'll throw out the first guy who says Wop or Squarehead." Sam got along fine after that and made peace between the factions to fight the cannery owners.

A traditionalist, Sam is proud of getting spotter planes ruled off the fishing grounds several years ago. "These days there's too damn much electronics—loran, plotters, GPS—no skill. My old man knew how to FIND the fish, knew where they milled up. That was fishing. In the old days guys would come up here wearing suit and tie. Now everybody dresses like slobs. Even (name withheld) over there, comes to this party looking like a bum. I know he's working on his boat, but the way he's dressed shows disrespect."

Soon the place is full of Italian fishermen, some with wives. I lose track of the Tonys, but have a nice chat with an Anthony (Russo) who is a sardine fisherman from Monterrey. In the *National Fisherman* several months ago I had seen an amazing photo of a big seiner in the Monterrey harbor completely covered with lounging sea lions. It was Anthony's. "There's absolutely nothing we can do. We can't shoot them, we can't even shoo them. We tried putting nailboards on the deck to keep them off, but the environmentalists even called us on that." Anthony had been 16 when he first came to Bristol Bay.

Uncle Squash shows up with his new crew, a no-nonsense little brunette in her forties. Somebody had circulated a lewd cartoon of a guy trout fishing and rogering his girlfriend from the back at the same time. Caption: "It doesn't get any better than this." One of the Tonys shows the cartoon to Squash's crew. She takes one look at it and says very drily, "I don't get it." Case closed.

Uncle Squash is a piece of work—a stumpy little guy with a fat belly and pants that don't zip all the way to the top. A widower, he still likes the ladies, but at 86, Squash claims he can't do anything about it. He first came to the Bay in 1932. Always had female crew. Crabbed in San Francisco Bay during the winter. Knew to the last claw how many Dungeness it took to trade for sex from the Rio Vista housewives.

We have a nice talk. Like many Bristol Bay boat owners these days, he was trying to sell out. "No future in it anymore." One guy put a thousand down on his boat last year, then reneged and sued Uncle Squash to get his money back. The judge took one look at Uncle Squash and dismissed the case. Now Squash has another buyer (who showed up at the party, very far gone in wine) who put $5000 down this spring on the boat. "Yesterday he tells me the hell with it, keep the dough. He's still drunk."

Kira, the singer from the Ponderosa Inn shows up accompanied by a couple of admirers from last night. She looks a little weary, but after much urging agrees to sing a few numbers, including one rollicking Irish folk song I wish I could have taped. Ron and Linda were right, she was a pip.

The food is served. Porcinos, salad, barbecued caribou and pork chops. Magnificent pasta. Great food and not a morsel wasted. We finally say goodbye. On the way back to Naknek, Ron philosophically tells us they didn't want to joint the co-op, they wanted him to buy their fleet.

CHAPTER 19

"Along about now, I feel like I'm playing chess in my mind on three levels."

The Wild Alaska Seafoods kitchen-cum-laundry room was a good place to sit and shoot the breeze.

I was down there having breakfast (orange juice, toast and a Snickers) on Sunday morning after the Italian barbecue, when Sam Daniel and his boy came in to do a little laundry. Despite his mild manner, Sam fishes the combat zone at Egegik—the westernmost legal line where the bravest, craziest and most daring fishermen liked to crowd in and set their nets to get the first crack at the incoming fish. Sam told me about the time when he and Ron had been "running partners"—the buddy system whereby two boats agree to keep track of each other. They had become widely separated on their way back from Egegik to Naknek in the middle of the night when Sam's engine failed and he was being blown ashore. (The airport anemometer topped out at 103 mph that night!) Even though Ron was many miles ahead, he answered Sam's call, roared back and went into the surf to pull him off. "What I like about Ron is his eternal optimism. That and he keeps his word." Sam's eight-year-old son was getting homesick and there was talk of sending him back to Girdwood. "One year too soon, I guess."

Ron Brill and Bob Smith come in next, looking considerably the worse for wear, but smiling and chipper for all of that. I reminded them of the English drinker's adage: "No gentleman feels well in the morning." They chuckled, but gingerly. "Has Ron said anything about when Lowrance is going to put the net barge out?" "No, but he'll be coming to the meeting this afternoon."

George Venarossa drops by. "Is Ron having that meeting this afternoon?" "Yeah, three o'clock." "Tell him I'll be there, but I won't be able to fish unless my new alternator gets here from Anchorage." George's boat was twelve years old, and stuff was starting to go wrong.

Kris and Todd come in. "How was the barbecue?" "Wild." "Are we going sport fishing tonight?" "Ron was talking about it last night, but I haven't seen him yet this morning." Kris likes to trout-fish and is considered both very good and very lucky by his father. We had been planning to go fishing up the river above King Salmon and tonight would probably be our last chance. "We'll be next door working on the boat, ask Ron if he wants us to have it moved outside to the yard. Oh, and the gen set isn't working."

Floyd comes in. He's been on the horn to Seattle and problems down there are still unsolved. The insurance scam on the *Akutan* looks worse than ever. In order to win his case in court, Ron will have to prove fraud. But now it turns out even if fraud *can* be proved, an "errors and omissions" clause in the policy will let the insurance company off the hook. Catch 22. It's all in the hands of Ron's attorneys, but now they want to get paid before going any further. Floyd hates to tell Ron, but he's going to have to.

Ron comes in. Still trying to sign up more boats and round everybody up for the final meeting. The cell phones are still not working and the new ones haven't arrived. Got to decide where to fish—stick around Naknek or go down to Egegik? Got to get the permits notarized. Was Kris drinking last night? Has Adams sent over our nets yet? And did Todd get the net tags? The hell with it, let's go to lunch. AND WHERE ARE MY FUCKING CAR KEYS? It's the little stuff that makes him nuts.

The final meeting came off as scheduled at three with about 20 boats in attendance including a handful of prospects and still-undecideds. Ron let them have both barrels which in abbreviated form went something like this:

"I'm Ron Peterson and I've been coming here to the bay since 1965 with my Dad and I've seen it good and bad ever since. Bought my first boat in '68. Fished for Whitney, then went independent in '78. Own the *Aleutian Number One*, a hundred-twenty-six-foot crab boat and have a half interest in the *Floodtide* with Ron Brill. I have a long term lease on this building with first refusal to buy and I own half of the yard with Chuck Allen. I used to be a partner with Chuck Bundrant on the *Dominator*, another Marco crabber. He tried to screw me and I beat him in arbitration and he still claims I rigged it which I sure as hell did not. I know where he's coming from and I know what he's trying to do here in the Bay. The processors are going to go limited entry. People laugh at me, but that's what's going to happen here and if you think it's bad now, wait till they get limited entry. It's already happening in crab and pollock and it's going to happen here. Our deal is different. We've got our own processing plant, Leader Creek Seafoods, and they've got a contract with Costco to take all the frozen filets they can produce. So you get on our A list and we'll take everything you can catch. No quotas. Get on the B list and if you give us twenty thousand pounds to start, we'll take everything we possibly can after that. We'll pay the average of the two highest prices in the bay. Nickle a pound bonus after the season. A-list boats get a two-point-four-eight-percent interest in Wild Alaska Seafoods which is my company that owns my interest this building and the yard. So you're guaranteed a home for your boat and your fish."

Five more skippers signed up.

Then Sam Daniel took over to review the details. The big sticking point is the tenders, which are to collect the catch from the gillnetters on the grounds and bring the fish back to Leader Creek. John Lowrance went to great pains to assure the fishermen that he had arranged very adequate tendering capacity—four tenders for sure, with one more possible. The skippers questioned him closely about the tenders. They were skeptical to the point of being chickenshit about it. They'd been burned before.

After the meeting Ron and Linda went to Mass held by a priest from Dutch Harbor who flies a regular Sunday route and hits Naknek at four. A little nap at five and Ron was raring to go to dinner and trout fishing after.

Linda stayed home and so all us boys piled into the Suburban and swerved our way down to King Salmon for dinner at Eddy's. It was a large and smoky, one-story-bar-cum-steakhouse. Full and loud. One waitress working at full gallop. The cook—a remarkably beefy specimen himself in a sweaty green T-shirt—knew Ronnie and came out of the kitchen to say hi. Todd and I sat at a separate table and I got a chance to hear a bit of his life story. His older brother has a band, the Newly Dead, that used to open for Kiss, the famous long-tongued, full-makeup group. Todd roadied with them for a while when he was younger. He told me it was a lot of fun, but they were totally strict about booze. One drink and you were fired. Period.

After dinner Ron drove us about ten miles out in the bush past the old Air Force Base along the river up to Rapids Camp where it comes out of Lake Ugashik. We left the road at that point and drove along the narrow shoreline another mile past a lodge with a few boats and a DeHaviland Beaver float plane moored out in front. We stopped, got our gear and put on our boots. Todd and Kris stayed by the Suburban and Ron, Floyd and I walked on down the shore another half mile. Ron packed a sawed-off stainless-steel twelve-gauge shotgun. "If you see a bear, yell BEAR!!!. Stop and face the bear. Yell. Wave your arms, make all the noise you can but don't run. I'll come and shoot it." The gun is loaded with three shells with buckshot and backed up by two more containing slugs. Ron has never had occasion to use the gun. But he wouldn't go ten steps out in the bush without it. The bank is about three feet high with meadows and scattered brush on a gradual slope above that. Plenty of cover for bears, but I am happy to report that we didn't see any.

Fish were another matter. The trout were big and hungry. Although I was very clumsy with spinning gear, I even caught one myself. Only about 20 inches but I never landed a fish that fought harder. Ron and Floyd both caught a couple. Kris and Todd were skunked.

There was a lodge across the river. Nothing fancy, but a fairly substantial house with a couple of outbuildings. Ron knew the former owner. This unfortunate fellow had been born there, inherited the place from his folks, but ended up forfeiting the whole spread a couple of years ago to the Red Dog Saloon to satisfy his bar bill. Talk about a tough place to drink.

Ron had lots of Red Dog stories. The worst he ever saw was a young drunk who carelessly pulled out his unit and peed on the floor. That wouldn't have been so bad, but he got some on the wrong guy's leg who beat him senseless and gouged out one eye before he was pulled off.

The Fisherman's Bar was another place to drink. "The bartender's name was Bullshit Bob, really big, really tough. I lent him fifty bucks one time, and he never forgot it even though he never paid me back. It was like an insurance policy and we were friends. I was sitting there one afternoon when a guy comes in and says, 'Gimmee a goddam beer.' Bullshit Bob didn't like the way he said it so he came around the bar and grabbed the guy by the seat of the pants and the neck and bashed his head against the door until he was limp and heaved him out in the parking lot. I followed the poor bastard outside and Bullshit Bob asked me where in the hell I thought I was going. 'I just want to see if he's still alive.' He was laying in the dirt, but still moving so I went back in to finish my drink. Pretty soon the guy came back in and sat down real quiet on a stool asked Bob if he could please have a beer. Which Bob gave him. No hard feelings."

On the way back, Ron gave us a tour of the King Salmon Air Force Base. Until the Cold War ended, it had been the home of a crack squadron of F-16 interceptors. Now deactivated, the entire base including eight fully-equipped hangars is still maintained in a state of combat readiness down to fresh aircraft fuel in underground tanks. Ron said he used to come to the base to watch movies. "I got along great with the C.O.—used to bring him crab and salmon eggs."

It was now about eleven and getting dark but Ron wasn't ready to fold. He wanted to stop at the King Ko Inn to see if Kira was singing tonite, but Kris groaned him out of it. So we drove around King Salmon some more. Went out to an oddly suburban neighbornood of about thirty modern homes nearly all of them empty. They had been built to house families of the workers who were to staff a proposed Federal Aviation Authority facility in King Salmon. But the project was scrubbed and the homes just sit there, only a few occupied. It made Ron salivate. "You can pick up any one of these places for five percent down, rent it to a school teacher nine months a year and have a great place to live during the season." Floyd didn't say much, only relieved that Ron didn't at this point have two extra nickels for a down payment.

As long as we were in the neighborhood, Ron wanted to show me a famous lodge outside of town. Couldn't find it. So he showed me a hotel on the river instead. It was now midnight, but we stopped and all went in, greeted the desk clerk and had a look around. The upstairs bar was closed but two old guys with their wives were still sitting there watching TV. It was a nice enough place, an acceptable 1-5 motel. Rooms start at $250 a night.

Ron showed no signs of slowing down, but drove us back to Naknek, talking a mile a minute, in excellent spirits. When we got there, I went down to the kitchen and snacked on a big chunk of rewarmed anchovy pizza from lunch and watched him clean the trout. Dylan Huff came in and Ron and he were still talking when I went up to bed and slept fitfully due to my pizza ballast.

CHAPTER 20

"Gimme that goddamn thing!!!"

Monday dawned snotty—windy with pelting rain. I thought Seattle weather was changeable, but it isn't a patch on Bristol Bay. By the time I had my breakfast—peanuts and fruit cup—it was clear sunshine. An hour later it was back to rain, but less wind. Like that all day.

The season opened tomorrow. Fun and games were over. And decisions had to be made. The first order of business was getting *Brianne Lynn* out in the yard and readied for launching. Kris and Todd had done what they could inside the building, but to raise the mast, put on water, start the stove and test run the engine, hydraulics and refrigeration, the boat needed to be outside.

Ralph and his boat wrangler were swamped with boat launchings of course, so Ron thought he'd speed things up by raising the "garage door"—a massive two-story affair—which promptly got stuck in the open position. As soon as Ralph showed up, Ron ran straight for him and confessed his transgression. I admired that. Having grown up with a testy father, I early grasped the wisdom of prompt confession of obvious sin.

Ralph fumed, but the door turned out to be an easy fix so it was soon forgotten.

While the boys worked on the boat, I rode down to King Salmon with Ron and Linda to drop off the fleet's "blue cards" at Fish and Game headquarters to register when and where each boat planned to fish. Also to drop off the "Permit Holder's Authorization" forms for all the boats designating Leader Creek as the authorized processor. As of Monday morning, the fleet consisted of eight "A" boats and six "B"s. Not as many as Ron and John Lowrance had been shooting for, but provided the fishing was good, the deal would still fly.

The ride down was unpleasant. Cell phone problems.

As previously mentioned, Linda had ordered three new cell phones from Dutch Harbor and more or less calmly took the attitude that she had done everything that could be reasonably expected to solve the problem. Ron seethed because he took the attitude—reasonable to him—that merely producing proof that new phones were on order was not an acceptable answer. This had been going on for several days. And it came to a head on the trip to King Salmon when it was discovered that the cell phone Ron *did* have—the one with the dead battery—wouldn't fit the DC adapter that Linda had obtained from the Naknek cell phone supplier, that bastard. This was discovered at sixty-miles-an-hour bombing down the highway, slewing wildly from lane to lane as Ron struggled to make the eight prong adapter fit into the six prong socket on the phone. I got it away from him to save my own skin. Not a pleasant trip as I say. Nor safe.

But we made it and Ron and Linda had calmed down and were pretty much at peace by the time we pulled into the Fish and Game parking lot. Not talking to each other, but not shouting either which was an improvement. I admired Linda's self control. She did not, at any point, resort to either tears or recriminations although in my view, most women would have, and indeed no jury, as they say, would ever have convicted.

The Fish and Game department was a beehive of activity. Ron was well known—and cheerfully greeted—by many of the staff. While he attended to his permits and paperwork, I studied the final run prediction on the bulletin board. Here's what I wrote down:

MILLIONS OF FISH

	Catch	Escapement Goal	Total
Kvichak	3.767	6.00	9.767
Branch	.226	.2325	.441
Naknek	4.425	7.315	11.740
Egegik	7.447	1.100	8.547
Ugashik	3.730	0.850	4.580
Nushagak	.212	.550	.762
Igushik	1.434	.200	1.634
Togiak	.591	.150	.741
Wood	2.432	1.000	3.432
TOTALS:	24,264,000	11,165,000	35,429,000

On the way back we stopped at a little place up the road and had a nice breakfast—full American—with fried eggs, sausage, toast, fried potatoes, juice and coffee. Peaceful, serene and filling.

The trip back was also reasonably calm but I noticed as we got out of the car at Leader Creek that Ron's thrashing around had broken the spine of the driver's seat which now slumped in defeat.

The rest of the day was a blur of furious activity. Getting nets. Putting the food on board. Talking to Lowrance—only one tender, the *North Wind,* had showed up so far. Working on the boat. Taking care of a thousand and one last-minute details. Including finally getting a couple of cell phones that worked.

The fourth member of the crew—Arne Vestad—was coming in from Seattle that afternoon and Floyd drove down to pick him up. Arne—pronounced *Arneh*—turned out to be a compact little Norseman, round-faced with crew-cut blond hair with a quite pronounced Norwegian brogue. An ace engineer, he had fished just about everywhere on just about every kind of boat up to huge catcher-processors. But he had never done Bristol Bay, so Ron wanted to show him what he was trying to do and maybe get Arne to help him set up a processing line on the *Akutan* providing he ever got that situation straighted out.

We were all out messing around with the boat when Chuck Allen came over to tell us about his intruders the night before. It seems Chuck surprised a couple young buckos trying to run off with his Honda ATV around three in the morning. A light sleeper, Chuck heard them trying to start the thing and slipped out with his 9 millimeter Magnum and fired a single shot in the air. One of them got away, but the other one stopped dead in his tracks while Chuck walked up and jammed his pistol under his jaw and gave him a stiff lecture "I noticed later that the spent shell had jammed and I was threatening the kid with an unloaded gun."

This was a big joke, but in truth, Chuck was not a guy to fool around with—both despite his age and because of it. Last year he had got in an argument with a younger man over a car deal. "When the guy spit in my face, I let him have it, buried my fist in his cheek up to my wrist. Then he went around town whining that I had blind-sided him. Then he tries to sue me for assault. The judge threw it out because under Alaskan law a man over 65 is legally the same as a child under 16 and can't be sued for assault. Last I heard, the turkey is down in Guatamala, sunk his boat, married a little 18-year old native gal."

CHAPTER 21

"Let me do the talking!"

Finally going fishing. I am up at five awakened by wind and hard rain After a little breakfast, (peanut butter and jelly on toast, Milky Way, tea) I pack my duffle and toss it on the boat. By 6:15, the sky is clearing and we are all sitting on the boat in the yard waiting for Ralph to come launch us. Todd, who'll do the cooking, has the food organized. Kris is showing signs of getting in a constructive mode. Ron is itchy, Arne a calm and reassuring presence. All is ready except for the diesel stove, which as Todd points out, is barely getting enough fuel to sustain flame, let alone cook anything. Arne is on the case. He decides the stove's impulse fuel pump is the problem. They send me over to Seattle Marine to buy a new one. Almost every boat up here has a Dickinson stove—made in Canada—and they're very reliable, but notoriously tricky to adjust. I had one on my own boat and it was a love-hate relationship resulting in many skinned knuckles and much bad language before satisfactory combustion was achieved.

It's only 6:30 and the store is shut tight. But another guy and myself go around back and pound on the door. Soon a light goes on in the adjoining living quarters and the manager comes to the door shirtless and zipping up his pants. "Come on in. Find what you want while I get dressed. The Dickinson pumps are over there on the back wall."

I go back to the boat with the new pump. In putting it on, Arne notices that there was no drain plug in the water tank. So we've got a couple of hundred gallons of water in the bilge and none in the tank. Fix that. Good thing Ralph hadn't got here yet. Arne continues to crawl around the engine compartment. His verdict: all the other vital fluids—oil, transmission fluid, coolant—are OK. Ron hires a local mechanic to mothball the boat every fall and except for forgetting to replace the plug in the water tank, the job was apparently done right.

With the new pump, the stove is marginally better, but still not putting out full heat. Arne turns his attention to the stove's carburetor. I have ideas, but try to keep my mouth shut. An All-Ocean Licensed Chief Engineer is on the case.

Ralph and the trailer show up. Up we're raised off the blocks and away we rumble through the yard and down the ramp hitting the water at 7:15. It is good to be afloat and away from the shoreside dirt and hassle which have gotten old by now.

We head out the river and Ron spots a boat he recognizes tied alongside an anchored tender. It's the *Shrike* and the owner is his old friend Pat Murphy—the one who broke the pike pole over his head years ago. Pulling alongside and holding position against the swift river current, Ron talks him into going on the "B" list. One more boat.

We make our first set at the mouth of the river at 10:15. A buoy is thrown over the stern and the net is pulled off the free-wheeling reel as the boat moves slowly forward. The floats astern show the position of the net tugged in a big arc by the current. After all the frantic activity, now there's nothing to do but sit and stare A bouncing float means a hit. A bunch of bouncing floats and splashing tails is what we're hoping for. But it's flat and quiet as we ride out the ebb. We see almost no sign of fish and neither does a sea lion who moseys along checking things out.

Ron has registered to fish Naknek, but is anxious to hear how things are doing 30 miles down the bay at Egegik where Konrad Schaad and Sam Daniel had gone the previous night. The consensus is that the fish are still far out in the bay, milling around before heading up the rivers. Some boats had done well yesterday here at Naknek but we sure weren't seeing much of anything so far.

It's now noon, still on the ebb until 2:00 and if there are any fish, they should be coming in on the flood. We see an encouraging bounce now and then and the guys are guessing 60 fish this set. This is just a get-out-the-kinks day. Arne keeps busy tinkering with the refrigeration unit that chills the sea water in the fish tank.

Arne tells me about engineering on the big catcher/processors. Their sonars detect fish up to 5000 meters away, 360 degrees around the vessel. Upon spotting a school, the sonar automatically directs the boat to the fish and steers the net to their capture. ("Look Ingrid, no hands!") The boats will carry a processing crew of over 150 people working six hour shifts. They'll do 40 tons a shift when they're really on the fish. Given their voracious efficiency, it's indeed surprising any pollock are still left in the Bering Sea.

We're still on our first set but have drifted miles out of the mouth of the river. I count 25 tenders anchored out to the west as well as several floating processors and a tramp freighter or two. The wind is gentle, the sky is blue, we might as well be yachting.

Ron is getting some well-earned shuteye in his bunk up forward There are four berths, an upper and a lower on either side of the bluntly angled bow. The head is just aft of the starboard berths—a plain aluminum compartment with toilet and washbasin with a shower nozzle on a flexible steel hose. Ron is insistent that the head be kept spotless—and that we wash our hands every time we pee. While cleanliness definitely counts, neatness does not; clothes and gear are scattered everywhere in the tiny cabin. This would be a very comfortable boat with two or three. But five is a squeeze. The stove and sink are on your left hand as you come in the cabin door with the pilot seat and controls forward of that. The table is to starboard with two facing bench seats, one of which just barely long enough to lay down on. Forward of that is a raised counter which is the ceiling of the head. The freezer box is up on the flying bridge and forms a base for the pilot chair.

This is a plain and utilitarian vessel, but I am impressed with the excellence of the construction—smooth welds, careful detailing, no rough edges. Beautiful workmanship in aluminum. This boat was built in Anacortes, but there are several yards around Puget Sound that turn out gillnetters almost identical in design and construction. Ron paid $100,000 for the *Brianne Lynn* back in 1983, but in the middle '90's, new gillnetters were costing $200,000 and up and permits were going for that much or more. This season (2000) they're below $100,000*

Ron rolls out around 2:00 and and at 2:15 and we finally haul. The guys are guessing 60 fish, but we actually only net 20. But they're beauties. Lovely, silvery, six-pound Sockeyes with the tinge of green along the back. The first fish out of the net is set aside—the traditional first meal.

I'm a little startled by the violence with which Kris, Todd and Arne pick fish out of the net. Using a tool like a plastic handled beer can opener with a blunt-ended prong. they tear the net from the gills of the fish and wrench it free. Many of the strangled fish are tangled in the nets and curled in a paroxysm of death. Not a pretty sight nor a peaceful scene. Freed from the net, the fish are

---

* *By 2002, the price of Bristol Bay driftnet permits had dropped to below $15,000, and one could buy a first-class aluminum gillnetter like Ron's for between 30 and 40 thousand dollars. At this point there are few takers for either permits or boats and lots of fishermen are going belly up and letting the banks take back everything. There's no way in hell to come out on 40 cent salmon.*

tossed into brailer bags hung in one of the nine bins under the net reel. The bags are about three feet across at the top and four feet deep, two to each bin. They're heavy brown plasticized nylon canvas—"No-Mars"—smooth so they won't damage the skin of the fish and with grommet holes around the bottom to allow the refrigerated sea water to circulate over the fish. After about fifteen minutes their bodies relax and lie flat.

We set again.

Around 3:00, the wind comes up and we get a stiff chop that bounces the *Brianne Lynn* around with a wicked motion that makes me a bit queasy. (Could it have been the Baby Ruths and salami I had for lunch?) I lay out on the deck in the lee of the house and feel fine after a short while. The sky has clouded over again, the sea is gray, the horizon flat and unremarkable—low sandy cliffs off to the north across the bay. This is not scenic Alaska.

Todd applies himself to making dinner. The stove oven isn't hot enough to bake the fish so he cut filets and fries them. Cubes some new potatoes and tosses them in a plastic bag with spices, onion and garlic flakes. Then sautees them as best he can on the half-hot Dickinson. The spuds come out on the crunchy side, but tasty.

Ron surprises me by saying a simple prayer before our meal, thanking the fish for giving up his life so that we might eat and hoping that the others that we caught will taste as good. Dig in!

After dinner we haul again. Three fish, count 'em, three. "Pretty damn scratchy, but that's why they call it fishing not farming."

Ron tells about one of the biggest hauls he ever made.

"Me and my Dad aboard my old fiberglass Rawson gillnetter back in 1975. We were fishing for Whitney and they were launching the boat off the dock with a crane. I always rode the boat down to the water so I could unhook it and run it over to the mooring. But as the crane was swinging me and the boat across I heard a crunching sound and looked up and saw the boom starting to buckle. I jumped over the side and knocked Dad out of the way of the boom as it crashed down on the dock. The hull just bounced, but the damn boom smashed the cabin, just demolished it. So after they got the boat shoved over out of the way, I figured that we were out of business for the season so we just went uptown and drank. But we came down the next day and the guys at the yard were jury rigging a little house with a steering station, depth sounder and a CB radio. A day later they put us in the water and away we went.

"We'd been drinking whiskey pretty heavy since the accident, so we decided to taper off on beer and fish across from Pederson Point—practically in the cannery's front yard. We were going up Albert Channel and suddenly we ran into fish so thick that it was like going aground, hitting the prop thump, thump, thump. We only had 75 fathoms of net so we decided to lay out right then and there. The fish hit the net so hard it looked like it was coming right out of the water. Scary. We loaded the boat with that one set—16,000 pounds—fish all over the deck, the stern almost under water. It was unreal. Good luck, bad luck. All part of the deal."

Ron heads in toward the mouth of the river and we set again. You never know—skunked one set, on 'em the next. An hour later the net is hauled and we get 20 more, all in the last 50 feet of net. Still scratchy, but not skunked. Set again, this time further in the river. We're a good mile off shore but it's so shallow we're plowing up mud. Ron is up on the bridge, roaring around, having the time of his life. "Let her go!" We bounce on the bottom four times as the net rolls off, tap bottom some more then go fairly firmly aground. "We do most of our fishing in ten feet of water or less." Ron pulls us off by hauling back on the net. A few fish, including a nice little halibut that Ron tosses over the side. "Save a life, get a wish." Set one more time, it's now 10:30. It looks like we're getting some action. Then the tender *Maverick* comes past, then stops and backs down to hail us. "Where's the fucking channel?" the young skipper running the boat wants to know. Then the *Maverick's* engine gets stuck in reverse and it backs across our net. Kris gets all red in the face, ready to blow up, having a perfect excuse to give somebody a full ration of crap, when Ron tells him firmly to shut up. "We'll get a new net out of it, let me do the talking."

Ron tells Kris and Todd to cast off our end of the net, then roars around the bow of the Maverick and picks up the buoy end, then goes astern of the tender—which is now hard aground on the falling tide—and gently tugs the net free—albeit with a big tear in the middle—and reels it in. Ten fish and a pair of nice twenty-pound kings. Ron is cool. He rather enjoys the crisis.

It's getting dark so we decide to hang it up. Ron gets on the cell phone with Floyd back at the office and learns that Konrad and Sam had hit it big down at Egikik—10,000 pounds for Konrad, 5,000 for Sam. That was the good news. Bad news was that John Lowrance's tender, the *Northern Star*, was nowhere to be found even though it was supposed to be there at Egekik. Konrad and Sam had no choice but to unload and sell to . . . . *Trident!*! "Son-of-a-BITCH!" And so forth.

By now it's completely dark and Ron heads up the river toward Leader Creek. It's after midnight. The tide is still ebbing and it's too shallow to get in so we slowly work our ghostly way through dozens of anchored boats, going as far upriver as we can but still about two miles short of the creek. Finally we find a spot in about four feet of water, toss over the hook, and like bats returning to a cave, hang back on our anchor line and turn in. "Son-of-a-*Bitch*!" Ron still fuming. It didn't help that Kris and Todd had wound the anchor line on the winch backwards. But that, at least, was fixable. Silence at last. Sleep.

CHAPTER 22

"Wake me if we get too close."

We get up at 4:30. Beautiful clear morning. The tide has turned and we have enough water to get into Leader Creek. Todd is standing up on the foredeck ready to tie us up when we smack hard into a rock and he goes sailing off the bow into the water. Much consternation, but before we can fish him out, he discovers it's so shallow he can stand up, which he does, and angrily wades ashore looking like a Sasquatch in his sopping oilskins. "Now I guess you guys understand why I always tell you to hang on with one hand when you're up on the bow." Todd flips us a bird.

We raft up outboard of a gillnetter at the bulkhead and Ron, Kris and Arne go ashore to get replacement nets out of storage. I stick with the boat. Our GPS has conked out and Ron has rousted out the local electronics (and cell phone) dealer out of bed to come fix it and wants me to be there to show him what it's doing. He shows up about an hour later—pissed and disgusted—and quickly fixes the unit. Ron had just pushed a couple of buttons backwards and it had locked up. "Tell that knothead Peterson that there's not a damn thing wrong with this GPS." "Stick around and tell him yourself." "No thanks."

Todd comes back to the boat. Having showered and changed clothes, he's in much better humor. Our torn nets—two 25-fathom lengths shackled together as one—are taken off, and four fresh nets wrestled on. The bagged nets are heavy. It's a three-man job to heave them from the shore to cockpit of the boat we're tied to, then up over the gunwhale into our cockpit. By the time Ron gets back to the boat and we get ready to cast off it's almost ten. The ebb has started and boat inboard of us is already completely aground. We're barely afloat as we cast off and as Ron attempts to turn the boat around, we soon fetch up hard aground on the far side of the creek. The weight of the extra nets in our cockpit sets the stern a little lower and every time Ron furiously guns us forward and back, we just sink a little deeper. The prop makes a horrible grinding sound as it churns up mud and rocks. We're stuck. Well and proper stuck. By this time all the commotion has attracted a crowd over at the ramp on the other side of the creek. "Toss us a line!" Ron heaves our little life ring with the light poly line. It falls short but one of the guys wades out and pulls it in. We use that to send over our heavy half inch bow line and that's tied to Ralph Young's loader. It backs up the ramp with a roar and pulls our bow off. Ron guns our engine furiously and we're afloat! Ah the joys of Bristol Bay tides. If we hadn't got off we'd have lost a whole tide—and a whole day's fishing.

We drop the two extra nets at Lowrance's net barge and are on our way to Egegik. I have fresh appreciation for the challenges of trying to fish and run a shoreside processing operation in an area with huge tides. Up here even the longest docks go dry at low water. Everything is at the mercy of the tides. Floating processors have a BIG advantage.

With the river current and ebbing tide on our stern we're soon out of the river and heading southwest to Egegik 30 miles away. Ron puts me on the helm and skipper and crew all turn in to get a little shuteye as we chug on along the flat, treeless coast at our sedate eight knots. Since the grounding in the creek, there's a considerable amount of new noise from down below—prop, transmission, stern bearing—it could be any one or all three, but it sounds like a sackful of rocks.

I sit up on the flying bridge and soak up the utter lack of scenery. The most prominent point of interest along this coast on my left is Johnston Hill, a long, low, rounded mound, several miles inland. At eight knots, we're a long time drawing it abeam and finally dropping it off astern. I usually have an exellent sense of direction, but the low featureless shorelines and the exaggeratedly northerly setting and rising of the sun on this, the longest day of the year, gets me fairly well disoriented. I'm as dependent on the compass for my bearings as if I was in open ocean. And like I was actually in fog, I have to fight myself to believe the compass. Odd hours, odder diet and fitful sleep may be taking their toll on my somewhat elderly self.

Anyhow, it was a nice three-hour interlude.

As we approached the Egegik area, I began to notice leaping salmon. First a few, then enough to wake Ronnie. We had just entered the northeastern edge of the Egegik fishing zone, a three-by-six-mile trapezoidal area extending out from shore and defined by Loran lines on the chart. I was sure that Ron would want to stop and lay out the net right here, but he had no interest in messing around with a backdoor set. He was going to the opposite edge—the Combat Zone—where the fish first enter the area from the open bay.

Soon we're there. The corner of the area is marked by a big 200-foot state fisheries vessel, and the three-mile line between the anchored ship and the shore is patroled by fish cops in a high-powered outboard inflatable. I count about 40 gillnetters milling around waiting for the 3:00 opening hour. The season is just starting so this is actually a fairly small fleet and mild showing for the fabled Combat Zone and there seems to be plenty of room for now.

While we're waiting, Konrad zooms up in the *Sluice Box* to apologize to Ron for having to sell his fish to Trident yesterday. It turns out that the *Northern Star* had actually been on their way down to Egegik and might have arrived in time but had made a leisurely stop along the way to take a few fish from one of the B boats. I began to see why Ron had been so concerned about having cell phones on all the boats—including the tenders and the processing plant. Sure, it's possible to do all the communicating on the radio, but the VHF is so much more complicated and time-consuming and everybody in the fleet can hear what you're saying. Cell phones are the answer. *Working* cell phones.

Airplane spotters had been another big advantage in Bristol Bay fishing, but as Sam Liberadi told me, they had been ruled off the bay several years ago. Ron, for one, hated to see them go. "Our fleet, Ocean Pacific, had a great pilot, Jim Blue, and five out of the top ten boats in the bay were in our fleet with Jim as our spotter. He'd spend up to 18 hours in the air and he had an uncanny feel for where the fish would be. He could read the water better than anybody. Had a head-on collision with another plane flown by a pal who was killed. Then six years later the same thing happened. Jim survived, the other guy bought it. No more Bristol Bay plane spotting, so Jim just gillnets along with the rest of us. But he still spots herring up in Togiak."

Bingo, it's 3:00 and everybody in sight is laying out nets for an eight-hour opening. But its soon apparent that there are more boats than fish—at least for the moment. We all drift quietly, keeping an eye out for other boats and other nets. Corking another guy's net is a screaming–bastard offense. With a calm sea and not too many boats, there's not much risk today.

We haul at 5:30 just to say we did something. A dozen fish. Lay out again. "George, just keep an eye on the net. Wake me if we get too close to somebody." So this is the wild and wooly Bristol Bay I've heard about all my life. Oh well, hell, I've read about it, I think I'll just relax and enjoy the peace and quiet. I sit up on the bridge and notice that Ron has broken the arm off the pilot chair. He's rough on seating, that boy.

That boat next to us starts seeing some action. It's an old

Rawson and his net, while not exactly jumping out of the water, is bouncing pretty good. They haul and I lose count of the fish they've got. A couple of hundred I think. More than we've seen.

We haul. Sixty fish. We lay out again, and the wind edges us closer to the bar. The sea seems dead flat, but in truth the combers on the bar reveal the existence of a big swell. Ron moves us gently away.

The "boys" are working together smoothly. Ron has made Kris the deck boss—he runs the hydraulic controls in the stern that haul in the net. Todd and Arne pick fish, helped as needed by Kris. More crew than fish so far. Ron tells me a story about the time a very depressed Todd was going on and on about his terrible childhood. Ron had him write it all down on paper and then burned it in a coffee can. Next year, Todd started his fugue again. "We burned all that last year, remember?"

We make three more sets with scant results and quit at 11. The sun is just going down behind us as all the boats in the area funnel over to the entrance to the Egegik River and steam up against the current to the anchored tenders like chicks returning to their mother hens. We pass our old friend the *Maverick*, looking deceptively competent. Then on up the line we spot our tender, the *North Wind*. We wait our turn, then pull alongside and tie up. She's a fairly typical 100-foot Northwest wood-hulled power scow. Pointed bow, house aft, big steel deck tank amidships. A line comes down from their boom, they pick out our two, half-full brailer bags. The scale says 1100 pounds. Not too shiny, but better than nothing.

Ron goes aboard and asks to see Dave, the skipper.

He shows up. An affable, heavy-set young guy, Dave promptly gets a firm lecture from Ron. It's not quite abuse, but rather more than advice. I watch this from our cockpit. The *North Wind* skipper starts out with an aggrieved "Who in the hell are you?" expression which gradually turns to incredulity and contrition as Ron explains life and reality in the Wild Alaska Seafoods fleet and where the *North Wind* fits in to the picture.

"And oh, by the way, Dave, would you give my friend George

a ride back to Naknek." Dave is not too pleased, but agrees and I grab my stuff and climb aboard.

Dave and Ron and I go up to the galley on the second deck aft. It's a broad and spacious area with a big sit-around table. "Sit down, Dave, and let's work out what you're going to need." says Ron. "Got paper and pencil. Good!"

The thing is, explains Ron, that the *North Wind* has to function as the fleet mother ship. With supplies and food and supplies that the boats are going to require in the weeks ahead. "First off, you'll need a freezer. Could you put one up in the bow?" The engineer is called up and yes, there's room in the bow shelter for a top-loader and they could wire it in easy. "Great, we'll send one up from Naknek. Now here's what you're going to need."

Ron prepares a soup-to-nuts list of food and supplies down to and including 20 half-gallon jugs of Clorox for sterilizing the brailer bags. By the time he's done, Dave and he are buddies. They shake hands, Ron climbs back on the *Brianne Lynn*, they cast off and head up the river to anchor for the night while the crew of the tender gets ready to raise anchor and head back to Naknek to deliver the day's catch.

I notice some left-over rice and pasta sauce on the stove and poach myself a little dinner. There's a nice long settee on the bulkhead next to the galley. I spread out my bag, climb in and am cradled in dreamland after tossing and turning for perhaps 60-seconds.

CHAPTER 23

"Oh, so you're Linda's boyfriend."

After four blissfully solid hours of sleep, I awake to a beautiful sunlit morning with a sparkling calm sea as the *North Wind* rumbles its way back to Naknek.

I wander up to the bridge. These classic power scows are such lovely old tubs. Wide and shallow with big twin diesels down below on the main deck. Dave is on the helm and tells me its history: Built during World War II, it didn't figure to last for almost 60 years, but, by God, here it was. It had been sunk at Bella Bella in 1993, then raised and righted and towed to Lake Union in Seattle where Dave and a partner had bought it cheap. "We filled 35 dumpsters with crap off this boat cleaning it up. Rebuilt everything. Five miles of new wire." It was certainly in nice shape now, everything well-used, but workboat-strong and tidy. Dave and his partner and one-man, one-woman crew had tendered in Sitka in the spring, came north to Togiak for the herring last month, and now were in Bristol Bay for Sockeye. They'd head to Southeast after this for the pinks.

"I just got on the boat yesterday morning, flew up from Seattle.

We were heading on down to Egegik when we stopped to take the fish off one of the boats on our list. That's what made us late, all right. Hell, we thought we were doing everybody a favor. Oh well. That Peterson is a character, isn't he?" "Oh yes."

There is low mist on the river as as we swung into the Naknek and head toward the fuel dock. It was 5:45 when we tie up. John Lowrance meets us. I heave my stuff in his pickup and we charge off to give Ron's supply list to Floyd at Leader Creek who had been warned to get ready for a hurricane-force shopping trip. (The *North Wind* would have to unload fish, refuel, load Ron's supplies and be on its way by 9:30, OR go aground and miss another day at Egegik!)

I go over the list with Floyd. "A freezer?" "Yeah, Ron says they've got them at the Trading Company. Get the biggest they have." Floyd grabs the list and tears off. As a former grocery-store owner, he's the right man to handle the job.

Me, I was heading home this afternoon, so I take my shower, do my laundry, have a decent breakfast and relax for an hour talking to Linda. She was bored, but filled her time by sewing and socializing—making new clothes and new friends. "All Floyd does is listen to religious radio. I've got to get out of here." (By the time Ron got back four weeks later, he said, "When I'd go around Naknek with Linda, people would say, 'Oh, so you're Linda's boyfriend.' She made more friends in a month than I made in 35 years. 'Course, she moves in a little different circle.")

Floyd comes back at 8:30 with the news that everything had been purchased, driven to the boat and loaded aboard. One more chore: pick up the replacement propeller at the shop out in the yard. And, oh yeah, be sure to get a prop puller too. So we do that and tear back up to the gas dock. The *North Wind* had just pulled out—it had been within an eyelash of going aground. But there was a gillnetter just heading out and the skipper offers to ferry the prop out to the tender on his way.

There. All done. Floyd had pulled a real coup getting all that stuff—incuding a freezer—bought and delivered just in time. The bill was over five thousand bucks. "P.A.F." Pay After Fishing.

Linda drives me down to King Salmon. She liked it up here and she didn't like it up here. An adventurous woman, hard to daunt, but not all that easy to please either. And why should she be?

I had a connecting 11:20 flight to Anchorage on a little PennAir commuter jet. It comes in carrying that day's allotment of lower-48 sportfishermen, many of them sheepishly decked out head to toe in spanking new outfits from Eddie Bauer and Orvis. Their guides were there to greet them, happily reeling in their fresh meal tickets. "Welcome to King Salmon, Mr. Bucks, I've got the van right outside."

My flight home is uneventful and pleasant. Egegik to Ballard in one day. What a world.

Next morning the phone rings and it's Ron. "Hey George, we just got a thousand fish on our first set. Call you later."

CHAPTER 24

"It's all about money."

About three weeks later I got another call from Ron. He and Linda got in late the night before and her car had a dead battery and could I give him a ride to Aki's Auto Rebuild in Ballard to pick up his Cadillac? It was a bright sunny morning in Seattle and there he was standing out in our south parking lot in shorts, t-shirt and flip flops calling me on his cell phone. I waved to him through the window and said sure.

He was in typically good spirits although the season had been a disappointment. He told me about it on the way:

"Things were getting light at Egegik and they moved the line in so far that basically it was just on the flats—at low tide there's nothing there. So I decided to move the fleet and the tenders up to Nushagak and I had to get twelve boats and the two tenders up there in one day. Sam and Conrad were sore at me because they wanted to go down the line to Ugashik, but it was too late for Ugashik and going north saved our bacon. The Egegik run was about half of the prediction and Ugashik turned out to be the biggest run they've had in a long time. We picked up a new guy

who knows that river real well—Mike Holm and the *Amy Marie*—
and it was fun. It's a big river and even with maybe five hundred
boats up there it worked out OK."

The catch of the Wild Alaska Seafood fleet finally topped out
a little over 800,000 pounds—far short of the 2,000,000 pounds
that Ron and John Lowrance had been banking on. That sounds
like a lot of fish. But at 45 cents a pound, it's slim pickings
compared to the glory years.

"We probably missed out on around fifty-thousand pounds
because the tenders started out so unreliable. The *North Wind*
went aground high and dry that next day after you were on it and
so we lost another whole day with that. The guys stuck with us
and waited but we could have lost the whole fleet easy right there.
And two days later I had engine trouble that could have cost my
own whole season. The aftercooler went out and we had to idle
all the way back to Leader Creek just pouring out pure black
smoke, right on the edge of ruining the engine. The other guys
accused me of dropping out just to go see Linda, but it was serious.
Thank God for Arne. The Cummins guy at Naknek had the parts
and Arne tore the aftercooler down and fixed it. As it was we only
lost four days."

I asked him about the bent prop and he told me that they
had beached the boat and put it on down at Egegik, but the shaft
was pretty bent too and he was unsure whether that had happened
in the Leader Creek grounding or the previous year. "That's Bristol
Bay fishing, and the boats have to be able to take it." Ron told
me about napping in his bunk one Combat Zone afternoon several
years ago when he got rammed so hard that there was a three foot
slash on the bow which poured water right on top of him.
"Aluminum is great stuff for a boat—just pound it out as much
as you can, plug it up with towels or whatever and get it welded
when you have a chance. Keep fishing."

We got to Aki's Auto Rebuild where Ron was a star customer.
Between his own fender benders and those of ex-wife Gloria's,
the Peterson account was like an annuity for the Aki brothers.
Ron also sweetened the relationship with frozen crab or smoked

salmon. Whenever he brought in a car, he made it a point to bring plenty of fish for the whole crew, not just the proprietors. His black Cadillac looked splendidly new.

When I saw Ron a week later over at his office, he was still remarkably jaunty. Floyd had quit the week before. Just up and walked off. Apparently he was so discouraged about Ron's situation and the constant dunning phone calls, he couldn't take it anymore. The office was a paperwork shambles, desks piled high with papers and records of all kinds—unpaid bills, unopened bills, uncompleted loan applications, unanswered calls—the works. Ron had been rising early and going to bed late to get caught up. Interrogatories on his lawsuits, permit documents, paying wages and settling accounts as best he could. "I gotta hire an accountant."

On top of that, Gloria and her lawyer had recently gotten wind of the house sale and demanded a whole new deal on the divorce besides her half of any house sale proceeds. Ron's own attorney couldn't handle the renegotiation because he had recently been disbarred for romantic pecadillos with a client. "That all happened years ago and even though he quit drinking, made it up with his wife and is a reformed character, they still disbarred him. So here I am with a couple of boxes of divorce papers it would cost at least ten grand for an attorney just to read it all and get up to speed. So I decided to do it myself without an attorney. It has to be a good deal for both parties. So I LAID IT ALL OUT AND THEY BOUGHT IT. But it took a lot out of me."

The upshot: Ron could go ahead and sell the house, give Gloria her share and have enough money left over—he hoped— to pay for his brown crab permits which he had "bought" two years ago but didn't have to pay for until this fall. (Price: $166,000.)

So, what the hell, Ron was still afloat. He thought he finally had a deal on the house with a couple of guys. But it fell through because they got into a squabble about how to remodel the kitchen. Then another buyer showed up. A divorced woman who had a lot of money coming, but not quite in hand. But that finally jelled and Gloria got most of the money.

The *Akutan* was still costing him five grand a month for moorage, and he still owed money up and down the waterfront, plus his lawyers, plus Gloria's maintenance, eight grand for landscaping and gardening bills on the house, plus, plus, plus a lot of other minuses in the cash flow.

He was trying to refinance the A-1 again, but stirring up the bank just caused them to try to call his loan. He had a confrontation with the special credit guy. "He's a big bruiser from Montana, doesn't know anything about fishing, just kept saying they wanted their money right now. I kept telling him about how valuable our brown crab permit was, and how I was one of the few crab boats that had a chance to make it. And he kept saying, 'Yeah that's all well and good, but we want our money.' So I finally told him, 'OK, fine, take the goddamn boat. You can have it. But the brown crab permit has my name on it and that goes with me, not the boat.' Jostein was in the meeting and he about swallowed his gum, but I told him, 'Jostein you've just got to go to the mat with these guys.' So they backed off."

Finally Ron got a personal loan from an old friend in Blue Ridge. "It beats the banks. They want to tie you up, down and sideways. Ron Brill just lost an injury judgment on one of his crab boats and the upshot is the banks are threatening to take both of his boats plus his house on Lake Sammamish."

Despite his precarious finances, Ron found another real estate deal that was too good to pass up. He took an option on three hundred feet of prime low bank waterfront on Whidbey Island just south of the little town of Clinton on Saratoga Passage. Real cheap of course. The waterfront was choice, but it had a steep bank behind it and the catch was access. The only way to get to the piece was through a private driveway owned by a neighbor who wanted to block the sale to prevent development. "I found out it would cost about two or three hundred thousand to put in a road down the bank behind my own property. But with the place platted into six lots and waterfront going at between two and three thousand a foot, I can sell off enough of the lots to pay for the road and have enough left over to build a nice little retirement place. Great clamming, George."

A couple of weeks later my wife and I ran into Ron and Kris at Ivar's Seafood on Lake Union. They were on their way to the Seahawks/Kansas City Chiefs game at Husky Stadium. Ron and Doctor Crealock share four season tickets. Ron usually gets all four in the later part of the season when the Doc and his wife go south for the winter. After we all got our orders at the take-out bar they joined us down at the streetend park next door where we talked and fed the ducks and one bum-winged Canada goose.

Ron was philosophical about Floyd. "I've talked to him since." No hard feelings but definitely another kink in the rope. Ron is definitely challenged but still undaunted. Kris was working at Penney's. He looked fine. Clean new duds—baggy white pants worn down at the lowest possible latitude. The stadium was on our way so we gave them a ride over. Ron was wearing his A-1 jacket and when we let them off, they jumped out and ran across the street, Ron with a huge smile and talking to people before they got ten feet past the curb on the other side.

As Seattle's fall oozed into winter, the *Akutan* situation was still unresolved.

Ron remained confident that he'd finally get his permit, but the banks, insurance companies and permitting authorities were definitely trying to run out the clock, hoping that Ron would cave in—sell the boat at a fire-sale price out of sheer desperation and walk away from the case. "The people that pulled the fast one on the permit keep telling me to be patient, don't do anything rash. The hell with that. I told those guys I'm done messing around, either give me my permit or we'll have to go to court. I know they don't want to do it because I'd win hands down." War of nerves.

As the days got longer and darker, Ron finally had to put a mortgage on his mother's house. She wasn't happy about it either.

Fortunately, the A1 had a pretty decent season on brown crab. Mark up one in the win column. The boat stayed in Dutch for the one-week red King crab season after the first of the year, then the short Opilio season in the early spring. Jostein and the crew fly home between seasons except for the engineer who's a Dutch Harbor native.

"I've learned a lot this year, including who my friends are." said Ron the next time we had lunch. "It's all about money. Most people have been real good to us, some of them have waited a year and a half for their dough. I tell them, listen, I've been through tough times before. Most people would go bankrupt, and I'm not going to do that. People have called me and said, 'Hey you owe us 70 thousand, what about let's just settle for 40?' I say, 'Thanks for your help, but I'm going to pay you every dime plus interest.' But not everybody in Ballard wants me to get my permits, they'd just as soon see Ron Peterson bite the dust."

They were disappointed.

In April of 2001, the *Akutan* tangle came unstuck and the permits were finally issued. And instead of a rusting hulk tied up to the dock, those pieces of paper instantly made the *Akuktan* worth a lot of money. Within three weeks, Ron sold the boat and permits for $1,350,000—the highest price ever paid for a west coast permit. "They actually don't even need the boat. The permits can be attached to another vessel and they may just leave the *Akutan* tied up or sell it for what they can get."

Bingo, Ron was over the hump.

CHAPTER 25

"I went from being the dumbest cluck in Ballard for buying worthless permits to the greediest bastard in Ballard for making them pay off."

Historically, the fisherman's worst enemy is himself.

At bottom the cause is "The Tragedy of the Commons" the phenomenon identified by Garrett Hardin in 1968. He wrote: *"Picture a pasture open to all. It is to be expected that each herdsman will try to keep as many cattle as possible on the commons. As a rational being, each herdsman seeks to maximize his gain. Explicity or implicitly, he asks, 'What is the utility to me of adding one more animal to my herd?' When all add one animal the commons becomes overgrazed and the resource collapses and all cattle starve."*

The "remorseless logic" of this phenomenon as it pertains to fishing was stated eloquently by Richard Adams Carey in his book *Against the Tide: the Fate of the New England Fisherman*. To wit:

" . . . that what you don't take for yourself now, when you have the opportunity, will be taken only a moment

later by your competitor; that if your competitor is taking
gambles . . . and winning . . . then you either have to
match his gambles, trump them, or be satisfied with what
he leaves you."

The Atlantic codfish provides a perfect—and perfectly tragic-case in point.

When New England was settled in the seventeenth century, cod were so abundant that at certain seasons settlers could wade out from shore and scoop them up in bushel baskets. As the years rolled on the cod fishermen sailed forth in ever larger and better boats with ever more effective methods of fishing. For two hundred years, the abundance of the cod seemed inexhaustible. Despite increasingly huge catches and growing evidence of overfishing, the Canadian government as late as the 1870's officially declared that the resource was indeed without limit. But by the onset of the First World War, the cod catch had begun a steep and undeniable decline. The Canadians of course ascribed this unhappy state to American greed and the Americans in turn blamed it on Canadian rapacity. When the war drove the fishboats of both nations off the North Atlantic grounds for three years, the surviving cod stocks took advantage of this interregnum to rebound astonishingly. This simple and undeniable proof of overfishing—and its remedy—was ignored by both governments and Armistice Day brought the fisherman back and the cod stocks again began to plummet. By the beginning of the Second World War, the Atlantic cod was again reeling under the pressure of overharvesting and after another wartime rebound, it all started again in 1946.

Today after years of factory ship depredations on the part of both nations as well as the British, Norwegians and Icelanders, the cod have almost totally disappeared from the North Atlantic and the species is commercially kaput. Overharvesting. That simple. Despite reams of rules and regulations. International conferences. Scientific research. All the brains and economic wisdom that the human mind can bring to bear. But the same result: Too many boats catching too many fish. Collapse of the resource. The tragedy of the commons.

Alaska offers further evidence, but quite a bit more complexity and perhaps a bit more hope. The North Pacific and Bering Sea are home to an estimated 40% of the world's stocks of commercial fish. And the permit situation in this part of the ocean offers a scene of Byzantine intricacy. To call it a tangled web is an understatement, snarled as it is in local, state and international politics, scientific uncertainty, environmental wrangling and plain old-fashioned greed and shortsightedness up and down the line. The Japanese, for example, now own the majority of the shore processing plants, employing local Alaskans. So this sets up economic tension with the catcher/processors, many of whom are backed by Norwegian money and crewed with fishermen and workers from the lower 48. Since the establishment of the 200 mile limit in 1976, which got the Russians and the Japanese out of the contiguous Alaskan waters, most commercial species have rebounded rather well. By and large, the state of Alaska is doing a good job of regulating the harvest, and very fortunately the remoteness and wildness of Alaska's rivers has preserved the inshore environment so vital to the survival of the salmon runs.

The bad examples are pollock and crab.

The Bering Sea has long teemed with vast, seemingly limitless schools of pollock. Although a species of cod, these fish are unpalatable unless cleaned and processed immediately. So traditionally, the pollock were totally disdained as a bothersome bycatch and the species went untouched. Then in the 1980's came the big catcher/ processors using ingenious midwater trawls—huge tubular nets "flown" through the sea at varied depths to capture vast schools of pollock detected by onboard sonars. They came aboard by the long ton, and were cleaned, fileted and frozen within hours of being hauled aboard. When the catcher/ processors first hit the Bering Sea, the pollock roe were fetching such a high price in Japan that they stripped the roe and threw the fish away—a lot more money and the ships could stay out longer because they didn't have to unload as often. Today, roe stripping is forbidden and the pollock fleet has a severely limited season which state and federal biologists believe will asssure the maintenance of the species at a sustainable level. But environmentalists disagree, pointing to the collapse of the Stellar sea lion population in the Bering Sea, blaming it on reduced pollock stocks, the primary food of young sea lions. Who really knows? Certainly the behavior of the sea lions is sometimes inexplicable. In August of 1966, some 60, healthy, apparently well-fed bachelor males jumped to their deaths from a 200-foot bluff north of Togiak. Shortage of food? Shortage of girl friends? Both? Again, who knows? (Maybe they just wanted to see if they could fly.)

The King crab fishery is another dramatic case in point. After the collapse in 1983 and after the state ran the draggers off the grounds, the crab have slowly come back, aided also by severely limited seasons. But there are still far too many boats after far too few crab. At this writing in 2002, there are still some 300 permitted boats in the Bering Sea red King crab fishery. Dozens of these are Seattle boats that still steam 2000 miles north and 2000 miles south again for just an eight or ten-day season. (Round trip fuel costs alone approach $20,000.)

Obviously very few boats make expenses. Very few red King crab boats EVER make expenses these days. Ron's old pal, Ron Brill, indeed has had to sell both of his crab boats—for less than he owed—and the bank is still after his house while one of his old crewmen is still suing him over the accident that happened two years ago. No fun. At this point, the authorities are talking about a buyback program to reduce the fleet by half. These boats would be taken out of service and absolutely forbidden to fish for anything anywhere on earth—they wouldn't even be allowed to work as tenders. But Peterson feels that reducing the fleet by 50% would still leave far less than half a loaf for the remaining red crab vessels. Letting so many boats into the fleet in the '70's and '80's was the mistake, and it was a classic case of the tragedy of the commons, aided and abetted by state and federal authorities who were anxious to please. "What difference does it make to add one more boat . . . . or two . . . . or a dozen." That's how Ron

Peterson got in, and in sober reflection, the A-1 was one of the straws that broke the camel's back. Ron says, "They left the door open too long. The government kept saying, 'OK, you guys, in two years we may not let any more crab boats in,' so a hundred more came in the door. Then they said, ' Oh well, we can't do it now, but two years from now we're really going to do it.' Then too many got in and it was just too late."

The irony is that Ron was one of the few that managed to survive. So here he sits with his Opilio permit, his red crab permit, his brown crab permit. The first two aren't worth much, but that brown crab permit is golden. Only 17 boats have them. No pot limit. A six-week season. Catch all you can till the state-set quota is filled. The species is surviving nicely and the price is great. Only drawback is the cost of rigging the boat for deep water crab. That and the fact that the state isn't giving out any more permits.

All this makes Ron look pretty smart. And many of his fellow crab boat owners mad. They called him a dummy to spend all that money getting the A-1equipped to go after brown crab. Now he's an SOB because he has made a success of it. To top that off, he went and bought the *Akutan*—a screwy old tub and a worthless permit. And the paper turned out to be worth well over a million dollars. That damn Peterson!

He thinks black cod will be the next species to go after with the A-1. He wants to lease black cod Individual Fishing Quota and pot fish down the Aleutian chain. Ron thinks it'll be a huge moneymaker. Instead of a weather-be-damned "Olympic" system where every boat has to go out and catch as much as possible in a short opening, the IFQ system lets fishermen pick their weather and supply the market steadily over time instead of flooding it with fish. Better price for the fisherman, fresh fish for marketplace. The IFQ system has been great for the halibut fleet. And better for the consumer too—here in Seattle we now see fresh halibut for months at a time instead of just for a week.

It all makes perfect sense to Ron, and he's going to go ahead on it as soon as the black cod IFQ 's go on sale. All it takes is money.

CHAPTER 26

"Once I figure out a proposition, I generally just go ahead and take the plunge. If I wait 'till I can afford it, it's too late."

As the year 2000 wore on, Ron and Linda seemed to be getting along fine. He moved his office to the apartment and was busy with the hundred and one details involved in cleaning up after the *Akutan* sale, paying bills, gardening his permits and lawsuits, dealing with crew paperwork and scheming new deals. The A-1 was tied up at the dock in Dutch after a good fall season and Jostein was home until winter Opilio, and things looked doable if not exactly peaches and cream.

The last big overhang was the *Akutan* fire insurance lawsuit. His attorney was crying about being paid and pushed the case off to a junior associate. Ronnie told them they wouldn't get a nickel unless they won the damn case, so take their pick—walk out and get nothing or help him win. "They kept pounding me for the dough, and I kept saying, whip me all you want, it won't do any good and as a matter of fact, I'm starting to like it." They stayed on the case.

Linda was good for Ron. Her cheerfulness and high spirits buoyed him through his low spots. But like any couple they had their spats, and these could be fairly spectacular. Linda wanted Ron to take an anger management course, Ron wanted Linda to be less exasperating. I could see both their points.

One evening in February, my wife and I were awakened about 11 p.m. by violent pounding at our door. It was Linda screaming "Fire! Fire!" I looked out the door and she was rushing down the smoke-filled hall to their apartment. I went back and dialed 911, gave my wife the phone and ran down to see if I could help. Ron was in the bedroom doorway throwing cups of water on their burning mattress and was a) buck naked and b) in a towering rage shouting at Linda that she had tried to kill him by locking him in the bedroom. She kept denying it, saying she had gone into the kitchen for water and locked the door inadvertently. Much, much yelling. A romantic at heart, she liked to make love by candlelight and at some point in the festivities, the candle had been tipped over and ignited the foam padding on the side of their new mattress. Ron gets very wound up when he's mad at Linda and kept repeating his grievance to her stout denials, both very loud. But no tears. I rushed out to the corridor and got a fire extinguisher and Ron tried to get into the bedroom to put out the fire, but it was so full of smoke he couldn't even see the burning mattress. He yelled for a flashlight and Linda found it and handed it to me and I shined it in the room, but could still barely see the the flames for the smoke. They continued to loudly argue as I went down the other hall to get another extinguisher. By the time I returned, I could hear the fire sirens and I gave them the news which calmed them somewhat. Both the fight and the fire were pretty much extinguished by the time the firemen rushed in, but the apartment and hall were still full of dense, acrid smoke. Ron was settling down a bit and Linda announced she was leaving and going for a walk. My wife told me later she had seen her go out to her car and slowly drive away. Ron had found one of Linda's silk robes and was lying on the couch gasping to get his breath. He said the room had been half filled with flames. And the firemen

confirmed that mattress fires were one of the worst to deal with—
they're supposed to be fireproof, but the side padding is
amazingly flammable. After a while, trying to calm Ron down
and pointing out that Linda was not as used to dealing with
emergencies as he was, I came back to our place and went to
bed. All in all it was a fairly hilarious fire. Nobody burned, no
damage except for the mattress. The smoke left Ron with a cough
that hung on for days.

Soon it was June and time to go up to Bristol Bay again. Ron
took along both Linda and her older son as well as Kris. Two
more different teenagers would be hard to find and sure enough,
the latent conflict between the boys caused problems between
their parents. After a week or two, there was a blow-up and Ron
sent Linda and her son back to Seattle. I've heard both sides of
it, and they both have a strong case. But it was humiliating for
Linda, and proved to be the end of the relationship. Despite
several attempts to patch things up after Ron returned from the
Bay, Linda moved back home to take care of her aging parents,
both of whom were suffering severe health problems. We were
sad to see her go.

The Sockeye season was another bust and the price never
got over 40 cents a pound. Boats were going for peanuts and so
were permits. Ron's old friend, Sam Daniel, was one of the
fishermen who was losing his boat—it was worth far less than he
owed on it, so back to the bank it went. After hauling the *Brianne
Lynn* out for the winter, Ron noticed severe corrosion in the bottom
plates. The boat had passed an insurance survey in the spring,
but apparently the contact between the hull insulation and the
aluminum had somehow touched off a severe chemical reaction
that rapidly decomposed the metal. Ron had the boat barged
back to Seattle for a new bottom. Another insurance hassle.

On a brighter note, there was money now to bring the A-1
down in August for a refit and a repaint. Ron had the work done
at a yard in Bellingham, and the day she was done, ready to sail,
he and I drove up to have a look before it sailed for Dutch Harbor
that night.

Ron was in great spirits. There had just been a last-minute settlement on his *Akutan* fire insurance claim. Less than what he wanted, but enough to make him feel good and clean up most of his big bills including paying off the loan on his Mom's house.

On the way up to Bellingham, Ron told me about a blow-up with Kris up in Bristol Bay. "One evening he waltzed in and told me he had decided to start drinking again. So I told him, great, if you're going to start, I am too so you better buy plenty of whiskey because I really like to drink and if I get started, we're going to need it." "Dad, you can't start drinking again." "The hell I can't, just watch me." That was that, the bluff worked.

So now Ron was even with the board on his big lawsuits and major debts. But he was still determined to have his pound of flesh out of the bank that sold him the *Akutan* for the deal they tried to pull on him with the permits. He figured to get either the bank or their attorney. Divide and conquer. "When the sharks are out to eat you, the only way to survive is to wound one of them and get their blood in the water so the other sharks will attack one of them and not you."

The yard had done a beautiful job on the *Aleutian Number One*—fresh paint from stem to stern, keel to mast truck. The detailing under and around every nook and cranny was impressively tidy and complete, not a speck of rust showing anywhere. Ron was delighted to see his pride and joy once more restored to glory. "I hated seeing it the way it was. It hurt to look at it." A hundred new 3-by-5-foot pots were stacked on deck. A couple of young crewmen were installing a new washing machine. They weren't the big deck-ape types of the old King crab days. Smaller pots meant smaller, wiry, tight-knit guys. Speed and strength more important than size. The A-1's young engineer was also on board and he and Ron had a talk about the season, the boat and the engine. "We really have to get that new main, Ron. Oh sure, I think she'll last the season all right, but it's about had it." Ron nodded, but when we came back up on deck he said, "They always have to take a run at me—new engine, new pots, new this, new that. Really need it? Sure, but they don't have to pay for any of it. I've put millions into this boat over the past ten years and haven't taken as much out as they have."

Anyhow, the boat looked great, but was in the usual boatyard shambles with stuff all over the deck and everywhere below. Jostein was driving up from home around dinner time, and they'd shove off as soon as he arrived. It would take them eight or nine days to get to Dutch Harbor so there was plenty of time to get things tidied up. In Dutch they would pick up more pots and their ground line which was stored in 40-foot vans. Keep going until all four strings are down, then pick the first one and away they go. The season began the 15th of September and they would go four or five weeks until quota is met. Then in October there would be a short red crab season, and possibly another short season for Opilio again in January.

I had lunch with Ron in early November and he told me the brown crab season had turned out to be a big success. The first set was huge and that was key. "If the first set is lousy, then you're behind the eight ball for the rest of the season."

October red crab was another story. Ron and I had talked about maybe going along for the red crab trip in October, but as it turned out, he got tied up in another permit hassle and I honored my promise to my wife never to go King crab fishing. So we didn't make it which was just as well. "They had a hell of a storm, on one boat a guy got killed and a couple hurt bad. It was a Marco like mine and they hit a wave so big that it just crashed completely over the boat, took out all the windows and crushed the roof of the after cabin. Just bent in the steel plates." And how did Jostein do? "Oh, they came through all right, but they didn't get a hell of a lot of crab. Only fished three days out of the eight day opening, the wind never got below seventy. It was a good trip to miss."

The National Marine Fisheries Service in Juneau was trying to take away his brown crab permit. "If they want to get you, they can always bring up all kinds of technicalities. I learned that when I was a company clerk in the Army. I'll get it straightened out, but it's going to mean more attorney fees."

His cranky aunt who used to own the gold mine in Alaska

had just died in Ballard. His Mom still kept in touch with her but Ron hadn't talked to her for years. She had been reclusive, suspicious and notably cantankerous, but it was going to be Ron's task to get her affairs straighted out.

While we were having our lunch, Father Gandrau, the St. Alphonsus pastor, came in with another elderly parishoner. Ron waved hello and the Father came over to see us as we were leaving. He had a crooked little smile on his face as he talked to Ron. I gathered that Peterson had been one of his all-star sinners at one point. But later Ron told me the Father had once told him in confession, "Is that all, Ronnie, I hear that kind of stuff all the time, haven't you done anything more wicked than that?" Ron said that Father Gandrau's eulogy at his aunt's funeral made her sound like a real nice person. He has a lot of respect for Father Gandrau.

In other news, Ron said Chuck Allen in Naknek is trying to help him buy the boatyard property at Leader Creek—the strip along the river that Trident had been trying to tie up. Ron and Chuck had the idea to build a new bulkhead out to deep water and fill in behind it. If he could get the property, Ron would get rid of all the old junk, put in a first-class boatyard and Naknek's much-needed cold storage plant. "Make a hell of a lot more money doing that than fishing. It was the guys in San Francisco who sold the picks and shovels that got rich off the Gold Rush. Old Sutter died broke. True fact."

Ron was also extremely tempted by the low price of Bristol Bay boats and permits. It's obviously the time to buy. He would like to find young guys who want to get a start and stake them. "Bristol Bay is going to come back. The price is down, but the world has to eat and that's some of the greatest fish on earth."

He hadn't seen Linda and she wouldn't return his calls.

The next time I saw Ron was just before Christmas. We drove over to a restaurant at the marina next door and as we got out of his car I saw a bunch of papers in the back seat with a cashier's check for $10,000 laying on top of the pile. "There's a lot of guys who'd break your window just to get a closer look at that, Ron."

"Yeah, that's my payment to Chuck Allen, got to put that in the mail today."

Ron was in good spirits, although he said he's been throwing up a lot lately. Flu? Ucer? Whatever. He said he has regular physicals because prostate cancer runs in the family and is what killed his Dad. But he gets a clean bill of health. I kidded him about eating right since Linda left, but he says he fixes himself three squares a day because he likes to cook and it isn't any different than when Linda was there because he did all the cooking anyhow. I do know that Ron eats a lot of seafood for breakfast, but I think that's just the Norwegian in him. I thanked Ron for the batch of big fat spot prawns that he had given us last week and he said he had a few of them for breakfast that morning.

Ron said he wasn't too worried about the brown crab permit. Just bullshit technicalities that can and will be sorted out by him and his attorneys. I certainly hope so. That one permit is really all he'd ever need to retire on—it could be leased to one of the other boats for about a half million a year and even after he gave 20% of that to Jostein, he'd have plenty.

His aunt's affairs are taking up a lot of his time. She had been posing as an indigent with food and household help from the church. But it turns out that she had money stashed all over her house (which she owned free and clear) plus various bank accounts. So Ron is trying to get it all sorted out for the benefit of his Mom and her other elderly sisters still living in Poland. He thinks it's going to be a lot simpler just to get all the money given to his Mom and let her send gifts (and an accounting) to the sisters rather than trying to deal with everybody's lawyers and tax collectors in both countries. Hassle for him either way.

Kris was still at loose ends. "I'd buy him a Bristol Bay permit in a minute if he was ready to work. But it's up to him."

Ron talked Jostein into going to Anchorage to attend the winter crab council meetings. Ron thinks this will be a liberal education for him. "It took me one year just to understand what all the damn acronyms stood for. Those guys sit up there and rattle all those letters around like they mean something and if

you don't know the lingo, they might as well be talking Greek."
Jostein (and his wife) have the feeling that Ron just sits down in
Ballard and twiddles his thumbs while Jostein takes all the risk.
"Be good for him to see what it's like at those meetings with
everybody out for your scalp."

I asked Ron about his Whidby Island property. He laid out a
bunch of sugar packets on the table and explained it. "This pink
packet here is the guy next door who doesn't want to give me an
easement. I've got two fifty-foot beach lots next to his and four
more fifty-footers along the beach with a thirty-foot wide strip
going four hundred feet up the ravine to the road above. What
I'd really like to do is buy all of the acreage up behind my
beachfront up to the road, maybe build a house up above. I'm
not really worried about the access. Actually this neighbor has
just bought his property and he can't deny an existing easement
to my lots. I might have to take him to court I guess, or worst
case, maybe trade one of my fifties for an easement But I'd really
like to own the whole damn piece up behind."

How about the Leader Creek deal. Still available? "Sure. All
it takes is money. Chuck is working on it and it's something I'd
really like to do." "So are you going to do it?" "All it takes is
money."

His main focus now is to lease as much black cod IFQ quota
as he can get his hands on. Ron spun figures out of his head
right and left about this IFQ. Of course these are amounts he's
been working with for weeks, but it's fun to listen to him dance
up and down the numbers—this much for the lease, five years,
first year recovery even if it was only half, add this, take out that,
what the hell, that's not a bad return, not bad at all. Big stare.

Ron says that he never waits till he can afford something
before he buys it. "Hell, all the stuff I got, the Akutan, the brown
crab permit, all that stuff, you know how much out of my actual
pocket I put up? Take a guess." I haven't any idea. "Ten grand.
That's right, ten grand." "I thought you had to come up with a
hundred sixty-six thousand for the brown crab permit" "I did,
but I borrowed it from the cannery. Worked a deal. Same with the

black cod quota. You can get the bank to lend on that. Or a processor. Just have to know what you're doing and not be afraid to do what you KNOW is going to work. Once I figure out a proposition, I go ahead and do it. I don't wait till I can afford it or until I read in the Fisherman's News that it's a good deal. If I wait till I have all the money, it's too late. I get myself in pretty deep that way, but I've always been able to get out. Like right now I've got to come up with a hundred grand before January first, but I'll do it somehow. It's a lot less than being four million in the hole, but it's still a hole and you have to work to get out of it. Same deal, just different amounts. I'm going to see my lawyers again this afternoon. Now they're laughing about my deals, but they didn't think it was very funny at this time last year."

"The boat is like a farm," says Ron, "And you have to force yourself to be optimistic. It's what you do and you better learn to like it. Motivate yourself. Never quit. As long as you keep getting up you're still in the fight."

Ron said that Jostein wasn't too happy about the black cod idea . . . him having to skipper the boat over a long season. "It's pretty sweet now, brown crab for a month, a week or two for red and Opilio, the rest of the time at home. But hell, I'll take some trips and we can get another skipper to fill in. Jostein makes money when the boat fishes, just like I do. Same way when we went with the brown crab. We had to get a crew that was willing to stay out there and work a longer season. There's lots of guys who will do it."

Ron's probably right. As long as God keeps making fish, he'll keep making fishermen. And when he gets around to it, he might even rear back and make another Ron Peterson. His call.

· · ·